THE TAPESTRY OF LIFE

40 ENCOUNTERS THROUGH THREAD AND LIGHT

BAHAREH AMIDI

Dedicated with respect to the millions of artists who have created handmade rugs for so many centuries without even having their names signed on the back or being fairly compensated.

And also, to the soul of my father who always appreciated such beauty. The rugs and tapestries in this book are samples of his collection at the Medallion Rug Gallery that he started over 40 years ago.

با احترام، تقدیم به میلیون‌ها هنرمندی که در طول قرن‌های متمادی فرشهای دستباف را خلق کرده‌اند بدون اینکه حتی نام آنها در پشت اثر درج شده باشد یا حتی دستمزد عادلانه‌ای نصیبشان شده باشد.

و همچنین تقدیم به روح پدرم که همیشه قدردان این زیبایی‌ها بود. فرش‌های این کتاب نمونه‌هایی از مجموعه وی در گالری فرش مدالین است که بیش از ۴۰ سال پیش شروع به کار کرده است.

Contents

Introduced by: Dr. Deborah Lindsay Williams	6
Prologue: The Tapestry of Life	8
The Artist in the Window	11
Piano Teacher and Holder of Secrets	14
Painting and Writing in the Moment	17
Meeting Frank on the Sidewalk in Frankfurt	20
Harry and the White Cane	25
A Big Moment With Mandela	31
Poetry Therapy With Ritha	37
Tapping by the Sea	57
Who Would Have Thought Tweeting Could Lead to Lida	60
Vera: Meetings in the Sky	63
Meeting the Poet Who Dared to Bungee Jump	66
Filipino Safe House	69
The Power of Art and Poetry: Meeting Larry	73
Meeting Neshat - The Reality of Words Touching Hearts	80
A Moment on the Sidewalk	82

The Smile Behind the Search	85
Car Wash Encounter	91
Shafana and the Prayer Beads	96
Pigeon Mail: Express Delivery	101
Meeting Mother and Baby by Taxi Stand	117
The Lost Children in the Park	123
What a Simple Elastic Can Do	126
The Beautiful Smile: The Chipped Tooth	129
Vahid by the Sea	132
Young Wise Teacher	134
Meeting Saffron	137
Meeting Khadija Through My Website	140
The Ice Cream in the "Not Allowed" Space	142
The Singing Lady Who Had So Much to Say	147
The Picture Perfect Story	151
Hebe From Sudan	159
Six Year Old in the Construction Zone	165
Claire by the Sea	169
David in the Air	173
Sergio, the Man Who Maintains Everything at Valporaiso	181
Lizzy in the Taxi	187
Mahara, Who Lit a Candle in My Heart	191
The Cat in the Bag	195
The Daughter I Did Not Know	198
Twins, Born Years Apart	201
With Deep Gratitude	204
Biography	206
Index of Rugs & Tapestries	208

INTRO BY...

Dr. Deborah Lindsay Williams is an affiliated faculty member at New York University Abu Dhabi. From 2015-2018, she served as Program Head of Literature and Creative Writing at NYUAD. Until 2010, Williams was Director of Honors and Professor of English at Iona College.

───────── In one of the encounters Bahareh describes in this collection, she talks about cutting open an apple in half along its diameter rather than down the length of the stem. She explains that when you cut the apple that way and it falls open, the seeds inside form the shape of stars.

As she tells the story, the star-seeds inside the apple become metaphors to describe the inner self, but I think the image of the star-seeds might also be a way to describe the collection of moments that are contained in this book. Bahareh is a woman of many gifts and one of those gifts is the ability to connect with the people the rest of us might dismiss—the bathroom attendant with a chipped tooth, a tattooed man on the beach, a little boy in a restaurant. Her interactions with these people reveal the star-seeds inside them and thus help us consider what might lie inside ourselves as well.

When Bahareh lived in Abu Dhabi, we walked together once a week along the Corniche or along the Saadiyat Beach, and I always came away from those walks with a renewed sense of optimism about the world. That optimism is not the false smile of good cheer; Bahareh is fully aware of the darkness in the world, as some of the encounters in this book reveal. No, the optimism you'll find in this book comes from a stronger and more real place, precisely because it has seen darkness. It takes tremendous strength, given the tumult in the world these days, to resist cynicism or ironic despair, and to choose instead the search for light.

What these encounters show us, of course, is that light is all around us, if we can just open our eyes. The American writer Edith Wharton once said, "There are two ways of spreading light: to be the candle or the mirror that reflects it." I think that this book serves as both mirror and candle, lighting and reflecting the world around us in such a way that we see it differently.

You can wander through these stories following any path you'd like, just as you might trace the pattern on one of the beautiful rugs pictured in the book. This book asks that you make it your own: define the starting and ending points as you like. After you've read a few of these encounters, take their spirit with you out into the world and let yourself be open to encounters of your own. That open spirit is the gift of this book.

PROLOGUE: The Tapestry of Life

The colors, the texture, the weaving, and the knots. This is how it all started: one coincidental chance meeting. There are forty stories that make this tapestry; there are dozens and perhaps hundreds of others that have come and gone, and those not yet revealed.

Here I share with you some of the beautiful moments of life that have revealed themselves to me as chance encounters. In each, there has been a vivid revelation and realization, from the white cane that showed me the way of life to the cat in the bag who has helped me see. It is through the threading of each of these stories together that I sit here now.

In each moment as life reveals itself, we are able to *see* or to let the moment pass by. Join me in seeing how moments realized have so much to tell and so much to give.

Each of these stories are real and true. I have changed the names of the people, but the characters, the thoughts, and the gifts that were given to me through the chance encounter all remain real and true.

Please help me weave the next part of this tapestry by sitting with me for a while, reading these stories, listening to them, and sharing them. Simple and real. Perhaps, but just perhaps, you will start to see how in your own life a chance encounter has changed your life. Perhaps you will take a moment to say hello to someone you may not have otherwise, on a bus, on the sidewalk, on a plane or just passing by.

Thank you for passing by. Touch this tapestry full of color, full of texture, full of revelations revealed just through a simple hello, a simple smile.

The Tapestry of Life—

The colors, the texture, the weaving, and the knots. This is how it all started. One coincidental chance meeting. There are no stories that make this tapestry, there are dozens and perhaps hundreds of others that have come and gone and those not yet revealed.

Here I share with you some of the beautiful moments of life that have revealed themselves to me as chance encounters but in each there has been a vivid revelation and realization from the white cane that showed me the way of life. It is through the threading who has helped me see. I sit here now, the cat in the bag stories together that I have. Join me in seeing how each of these

In each moment as life reveals itself, we are able to see or to let the moment pass by. And so much to give, seeing how moments realized have so much to tell and so much to give. Characters, real and true, I have changed the names Each of the stories are 100 percent real and true. Part of this tapestry that were of the people, but the characters, the thoughts and all remain real and true.

Please help me weave the next stories. Perhaps listening to them and perhaps with me for awhile, reading and read. Simple part of this tapestry and perhaps sharing them. Simple and see how in your own life, and perhaps a chance you will start to take a moment to your life, a soul hello encounter has changed how may not have otherwise to someone on the sidewalk, or a phone or on a bus, or the you by touch, just passing of color, texture. Thank you for pausing just through this tapestry full hello, a simple revelation revealed of a simple hello smile,

Balance

The Artist in the Window

Abu Dhabi – May 2014

I was walking in our neighborhood one afternoon, running a few errands and taking in the sights and sounds of the universe as I sometimes do. I saw someone sitting in a window, leaning over and doing something. Looking closer, I was amazed at what I saw. Of course, I went in and said hello. There was a young man sitting in the window of a flower shop in Khalidiyah in Abu Dhabi with his pen in hand, working on the most detailed piece of art I have ever seen. The horse in ink spoke to me. It actually did; the soft eyes, the gentle nose, the whispers I could almost hear.

The details were unbelievable. A series of dots, lines, and hand motions, making marks on paper. All of it together made an incredible piece of art. It was a nice space: cozy and welcoming both to me and to someone who could sit in the window to create. I started speaking to the young man, whose name I discovered was Elmo. He said he worked in the flower shop, and in his spare time, he picked up a pen and paper and created art.

"There are others," he told me gently as he started to flip the pages of his notebook. I stood, in awe of such beauty but also of the dignity and humility of the artist.

"Where do you show your art?" I asked him.

"I don't really," he replied. "I just do art on the side when I get a break from my work. I paint as well. Would you like to see a few of my pieces?"

I was delighted at this offer. He disappeared upstairs and came back with one, then another, then yet another magnificent piece. The incredible thing for me was the variety of both subject and styles and strokes.

Elmo told me he had never taken any art classes and had always done it because he enjoyed it. It shone through in his work, and his soul was filled with colors and textures, pen strokes and ink.

As he did not have anywhere to display his creations, Elmo had all of his pieces tucked away. He showed me where he painted in the attic of the flower shop during his lunch breaks. He was an artist at heart whose soul was fed by his work and whose art

could feed the souls of others.

Days, weeks, and months passed. I would visit Elmo from time to time, and each time I was more amazed at his art and at his heart. Conversations led to me writing to a friend that worked at a newspaper. She contacted Elmo, interviewed him, and presented his work in a beautiful way. He needed to be admired and showcased.

Shortly afterwards, Elmo showed his art at a beautiful studio of art, yoga, and meditation. When I visited him another time, he gifted me with an oil painting and one of his inks. The oil painting, which is of flowers in a garden, brings joy to my life each day. The ink piece is the most delicate impression of a horse's profile: each hair could be seen and felt.

For me, my friendship with Elmo has brought such cheer to my life. Through a window, in a looking glass, and all around, there are such divine beauties every step of the way.

Piano Teacher and Holder of Secrets
Washington, D.C. – 2002 – 2007

My daughters were taking piano lessons from an elderly lady from Hungary. She lived all alone in a lovely house in a lovely part of town in Washington, DC.

She was always immaculately dressed, and adorned with an elaborate brooch.

She was very strict, but the kids loved her nevertheless. I sat there and listened and wrote and read during my daughter's lessons.

Sometimes, Mrs. Clady sat at her antique Steinway and played classical pieces before her lessons. Her fingers brought the black and white keys to life.

Slowly, Mrs. Clady and I started talking and spending more time together, talking about life. Over the years, I offered to take her anywhere she wanted to go, since she had recently stopped driving (Thank goodness).

One day, she asked me if I could take her to a doctor's appointment, and so I went and picked her up.

After the appointment, we ended up parking the car on the side of the street and talking. To be completely honest, she talked, and I listened, gladly. She told me about a love she had when she was younger. She had never told anyone about this love before, and she told me she loved sharing the story. I could feel the joy in her voice and in her eyes. What beauty.

I feel like I carry her secret, I know, I will let it carry on forever. She entrusted in me something that may have been as sacred to her as her grand piano.

After some years, Mrs. Clady moved to another state and stayed in a senior citizen home. I talked to her a couple of times. She said there was a piano there that she played from time to time, but she missed her grand piano.

Painting and Writing in the Moment

Los Angeles – July 2012

In the summer of 2012, I was in California, taking some Poetry Therapy courses and visiting family. I had gone to visit my niece, and she had a friend over. Her name was Lola, and as we sat down on the deck overlooking the golf course, we started talking. We had the usual small talk until I asked her what she did. This was odd for me, because at the time I had been avoiding asking people that question. It seemed like such a fake thing to talk about most of the time.

Lola said, "I am a painter." Even more importantly, she added, "I paint in the moment."

My nephew, who was sitting close by, said, "Oh that's interesting, my aunt writes in the moment."

This is true; I write about what I see and feel in the moment, as much as I can. I told Lola it would be wonderful to do something in collaboration with her, like me reading and her painting. She agreed.

We were in San Francisco at the time, but Lola lived in Los Angeles. I was going to L.A. the following week, and so we agreed to meet up and figure something out. It started out as me going to her studio, which at the time was in her garage. Eventually, we thought of inviting a few people and recording the event. We ended up on the rooftop of Ten Ten, a building where people can live and work and play, a unique space with positive energy.

There were candles lit everywhere, some fresh fruit, live music. There were some friends and some people I did not know, but the feeling was that of a moment of light and flight. We were joined by Hatam on the cello, Hamed on the santur, and Emily on the violin. Incredibly, Emily, who lived in Abu Dhabi, had seen the invite page on Facebook and contacted me. She magically appeared with the friendly violin I know well, and she and Hatam and Hamed started speaking the language that their instruments knew best. I am sure their notes and strings had met each other years ago.

As they were practicing, Lola started setting up her canvas and getting ready for flight. The fire in the background, the wonderful music, and the colors started to speak and the real magic began. We had also set out some extra colors and notepads for those who felt the call to write or draw in the Moment.

We started the evening with a poem I had written a while back:

The Moment

At any given moment

my life

can change

look at the people around me

each of them know one other person

and that person

another

who knows who

on the other side of the world is having the most effect

on my life

it can be me

my soul

you

the pope

the queen

or the sweeper

sweeping away the

moments of life

Meeting Frank on the Sidewalk in Frankfurt

Frankfurt – October 2015

——————— It was my first time visiting the Frankfurt Book Fair. I spent the days walking from hall to hall, meeting people, and picking up books, all while eating fun snacks along the way.

Each and every country was represented, and everyone was there side by side in peace and harmony. I had looked up a few interesting things to do before coming, and among them was a talk at the Iranian stand on Day Two.

Sadly, when I approached, the area had been completely taped off and there were no books. I was sad about the talk, but I went on with my time in Frankfurt and enjoyed what was there.

On one of my last nights in Frankfurt, I went out for a long walk. It was a cold night. I was wearing a light coat, a hat, a scarf and gloves, and it was still freezing. I decided to take shelter in a bar for the warmth, but also for some people watching. I spoke to one nice lady inside the bathroom, shortly after I entered, and gave her my card. I actually heard from her later, she is a psychologist and was interested in what I do. The rest of the night, however, passed without me talking to anyone else. It was not because I didn't want to, but because it just happened that way. No one approached me, and I approached no one.

Everyone was smoking there and so I felt like smoking, even though I do not smoke and never have. When everyone else is doing something, sometimes I feel like doing it too. I bought a pack from the bar and puffed for a bit before I decided to get up and go. As I got up, I considered leaving the pack of cigarettes on the table, but ended up taking them with me.

I started walking outside and it felt even colder than before. There was a man lying down on the sidewalk with only a light blanket covering him.

"Hello," I said.

"Hi."

"Do you smoke?"

"Yes," he replied.

"Oh okay, good. Here you go," I said, giving him the pack of cigarettes and the matches. He was so happy. "It's not the best thing to offer you, but since you smoke anyway, I guess it's okay."

He sat up, and we started chatting. He told me his name was Frank, and that he was used to the cold because he had been living on the street for 17 years. I told him where I was from, and asked him why he did not stay in churches or shelters.

"There is too much preaching and too much drinking," he said. "I would rather be on my own."

After a while, it seemed like it was time for me to go, and I asked if we could have a picture together for the memory. We took a selfie, which is one of the pictures and moments I shall always cherish.

I walked on with my head not quite on my shoulders; I had not yet reflected upon the conversation that had just taken place. As I walked, I came across a very happening place, with people drinking and eating and looking like they were having a good time. I was hungry so I went in. For 6.50 euros, I could eat all I wanted. The food was truly magnificent: the best I had on the whole trip. I had the vegetarian lasagna and rice and chicken, but the whole time I could not stop thinking about Frank.

After I was done eating, I made a plate for Frank with the same things I had, plus some cold cuts, cheese, and bread, and a coke. Bag in hand, heart full of joy, and stomach full of great food, I walked back to where Frank resided on the sidewalk. It was almost midnight, and even colder than before.

I found my brother Frank, there, in the same place. I told him where I had eaten and how I had thought he might enjoy the same dinner. I sat with him for a minute or so, and then said goodnight. I looked back and saw him wave, so I waved back.

The next night, I went to the English theatre to see the Glass Menagerie by Tennessee Williams. It was a great program, but throughout I was looking forward to walking back to the same restaurant for dinner. When I finally got there, it was rather dark inside, with none of the commotion and happiness of the night before. There were only a few people, and no food or anything. I went to the door and asked the security guard about the restaurant. He told me that there is only food when there's a show going on at the theater next door, and that it was only for the patrons. I realized that I had gotten in by chance the night before. Maybe Frank's angels wanted both of us to eat that food last night.

I walked around for a bit, disappointed, and found a hamburger place. I ordered a cheeseburger and fries and looked out the window. It was my last night in Frankfurt. I thought of Frank again, since he was close to this place, so I ordered a double cheeseburger and fries and drink for him to go. Paper bag in hand, I walked toward where Frank lived. His things were there, the small white blanket he laid on and the other he put on top of him, but there was no Frank. I took out a pen and wrote on the paper bag.

"To Frank, from your sister, Bahareh."

Harry and the White Cane
Washington, D.C. – 1990

As I walked down the sidewalk in suburban Bethesda, Maryland, the grocery bags I carried felt heavier than they usually did. I decided to take the free, local shuttle that most of the elderly people in the neighborhood used. While sitting on the shuttle, I overheard an older gentleman with white hair ask the driver what street we were on. A bit later, I heard him ask the same question again.

The shuttle stopped, and the questioning man got out. I noticed he was holding a white cane. Although it was not my stop, I got off, thanking the bus driver as I left.

"Hello," I said to the gentleman. "I noticed you were asking what street we were on."

"Yes, I have just moved to the neighborhood, and I need to get my bearings."

"My husband and I moved here recently as well," I told him. "I would love to walk around with you and get to know the neighborhood better."

"What is your name?" he asked me.

"Bahareh," I said. I could see on his face that this would be hard for him to remember. "But some people call me Hope."

"My name's Harry," he said, smiling.

We said our goodbyes and each went our own way home.

After that day, Harry and I went grocery shopping together once a week. I would walk to his apartment, and he would be waiting for me in the lobby. He was always so well dressed, his blue eyes shining from afar.

We would walk and talk and do his shopping, which I had gotten to know so well; the baby peas in the small cans and the same brand of coffee that never changed. Harry knew exactly what he needed and exactly what brands he liked.

Over the years, we shared stories of our lives. He told me about when he used to have his sight and what it was like when he lost it completely. He told me that at times, he could see shades or shadows, but usually nothing at all. He told me about his children and grandchildren. He told me about his first wife and their divorce, his second and third wives and their deaths. He was full of life, full of hope.

One day, we walked into the local barber shop that he had been going to, since his move.

I sat quietly watching the barber cut Harry's hair. They exchanged some niceties and every now and then Harry would check in with me to see if I was okay.

"Where did you pick up this good looking lady?" his barber asked.

"She picked me up on a bus!" said Harry. We all laughed.

That was the first of many visits to the barber, each time we all became more familiar with each other, knowing well that it was Harry's kindness and vision that had brought us together.

I told him all about my childhood, my family, my ups and downs. There were no masks to hide behind. Harry loved me for me, inside and out.

Once he had gotten more comfortable with me, he touched my face to get to know my features. He knew me so well without knowing how I looked. He could always tell if I was sad and would ask me what was wrong without pushing me to share. I always did.

It was an honor to have Harry hold my first child. He was one of the first visitors that came over and held my daughter, Ariana. She was a fussy baby, but in his arms she was happy. He brought joy wherever he went.

Some years later, he met the woman of his dreams. They got married and are still together, traveling the world by ship, by plane, by hot air balloon… but I think they mostly travel in each other's hearts. My girls and I would go to visit them and their enormous Christmas tree every year, enjoying the special cookies and decorations.

After Harry got married, we stopped doing our weekly grocery outings. By that time, I was busy with my own little family, too. Instead, we would meet for lunch. We would go eat the Persian kababs that Harry had grown so fond of.

From time to time, when it was his wife's birthday or on Christmas, he would call me up so we could go look for a special gift. He always knew what he wanted to get, and I was only there to help with the final choosing. All the scarves, bracelets, books, and slippers that he so carefully purchased were filled with his light.

I could not be more grateful for the heavy groceries that made me take the shuttle so many years ago. Meeting the man with the white cane has helped me see the world so differently. His light will always fill my heart.

A Big Moment with Mandela

Abu Dhabi – December 2013

The day we heard news of Nelson Mandela's death was a heartbreaking one. To have lived at the same time as him makes me know that I have been blessed until eternity.

A dear friend of mine told me, "Bahareh, why don't you write a poem for his memorial and take it to the Embassy of South Africa?" I went one day and sat for an hour on the steps of the church where the memorial was to take place. There, came the poem.

When I say the poem came, that is exactly what happened. I opened my heart and thought of Nelson Mandela and his life and then, as if in a capsule, the poem arrived. I did not have to change or edit in any way at all.

I knew I had to deliver it to the Ambassador, and so I did, meticulously presented and framed. The following day, I got a call from the Embassy inviting me to recite the poem at the memorial.

If I were to encapsulate how I felt for the wonderful, hour-long journey that was the celebration of the Nelson Mandela's life, I would say it felt like a deep breath. I wish I could take this feeling, with all the hope and energy and light it brought, and make it last for years. To be in a space filled with souls from all over the world, regardless of race, religion, or sex, who were all there to celebrate the single burning candle in the room was a feeling I cannot describe. Mandela's candle is one that will burn for all eternity, and its wax will mold into shapes and colors to fit all times and places.

Space and time stood still for that one hour, as ambassadors, representatives, and chairmen spoke, while infants cried. Time stood still as hymns were sung and everybody raised their voices in unison. The hymns celebrated *life*, with no exceptions for color or religion—simply eternal being.

There was a moment of silence at the start of the ceremony, which felt like a lifetime. It made me think of the hours, days, months, and years that Mandela's candle burned to make him the person he was.

When his Excellency, Ambassador of Argentina spoke and recognized Mandela, there was a huge round of applause and the entire congregation stood up. It felt like more than that though, like the whole universe had stood up and applauded the life of Mandela. No one could stop clapping, and no one would stop. Those vibrations remain in my chest to this day.

I would like to thank the Embassy of South Africa and His Excellency Ambassador, as well as the wonderful organizers for asking me to recite the poem at the event. I would also like thank the brothers and sisters that held me tight. I feel I am a child of the Universe, so I was truly touched.

Here is the poem I recited on this indescribable occasion:

Remembering the Smile of Madiba...

What does one begin to say about a person

who broke so many barriers, so many walls?

Nelson Mandela, to me, represents a human being.

Neither man nor woman; but both.

Neither black nor white; but both.

A person of religion, but more so a person of spirit and truth.

I can and have written volumes of verses about such a person,

but if I had to summarize Mandela's life teachings for myself or

for someone who may have landed in this gathering from Mars today

that message would be:

smile with your heart.

For in that smile

the heart sees no color, recognizes no walls, and hears no inequality.

Apartheid was not, is not, a thing of the past.

It is here among us today.

May we on this day of remembrance

open our hearts to no stars, crosses, or crescents.

May we recognize all who live at home as king or queen

regardless of the person sleeping on the king bed

or washing those sheets.

Each sheet of blank paper we see each day,

a reminder that it is us, it is I who will write the history of this tale.

As Nelson Mandela would say

not to omit the dark spots of one's life

but only to learn from each breath.

Perhaps it is in recognizing the decades of solitude and walls

that I truly begin to see the Light in today's memorial.

Remembering Mandela could see the other side.

May we see the other side of the coin

as we drive by a worker whose name may resemble his.

Dignity does not arrive in a suit and tie, nor a fancy car,

dignity and honor arrive with a simple heartfelt smile.

Poetry Therapy with Ritha
Abu Dhabi – March 2013

When we arrived at the room, there were two nurses standing on either side of Ritha. She was being poked for blood, and she was squeamish and unhappy. She recognized the kind doctor who accompanied me to her room and looked me over. I was introduced briefly, but the focus was on the blood, or lack thereof.

"They have been poking me so many times, and nothing comes," Ritha said.

I stood by the curtain for a while, and then I heard her small cries. I walked next to her bed and held her hand. I could not do anything but be present with her. I was becoming somewhat alarmed of the pokes and the cries of pain from Ritha, I stepped aside by the curtain, then the kind doctor asked me to step out and I did.

"Here, wash your hands and wear gloves. You need to be careful when there is blood," she said.

The blood was extracted finally. The nurses left, and we sat close to the bed: the doctor on one side, I on the other. The doctor explained to Ritha a bit about what I do. Very briefly, they talked about what Ritha had eaten (or not eaten, the lunch or dinner tray untouched nearby). Ritha said she did not like the food. The doctor talked about how Ritha would need her energy to go home, and that is when I saw a light. Ritha's face opened.

"When am I going home?" she asked.

I felt this was a cue. I took out three journals from my bag and paper and a packet of poetry. I showed Ritha the journals and asked if she would choose one. I held two up, then another. She chose one of the books.

I asked her if she would tell me a little bit about how it felt to go home. I wrote while she spoke.

> *Now I am going home....*
>
> *The hospital arranged it for me*
>
> *They treated me*
>
> *and they have been paying for my son's school fees*
>
> *And they gave me all I needed*
>
> *I love them so much. They gave me*
>
> *money to go home to my country to start my business*
>
> *They will not let me down*
>
> *And I will never forget them*
>
> *I had a restaurant and I sold it*
>
> *I agreed to work for a woman in Dubai*
>
> *in her restaurant*

When I reached there

I asked to go to the restaurant

The woman told me there was no restaurant

She took all my documents from me

and told me:

You are going to do as a sex worker

I was confused because in my life I have never done that sort of thing

She took me into her house

and she told me she wanted seven thousand dollars

She used to bring for me men

She brought for me three men in one day

and they forced themselves on me and they gave me money

Each one 100 Dirhams and the next time

I started bleeding

When she brought the men I said those men cannot be here I am bleeding

She told me even if you are bleeding

They have to be with you because I want my money

I refused and she left me for one month in the house

While I was bleeding

She didn't give me food

She didn't give me drink

When she saw that I was going to die

sleeping on the floor without a mattress, bleeding

She called the taxi

She took me to Dubai

and she threw me there behind Dubai hospital

The ambulance came and picked me up

The nurse asked the ambulance man

Where did you get this lady?

The ambulance driver told the nurse

I picked her up outside

The nurse asked me who has brought you here?

I told them about the woman

They started to scan me

They removed blood from me

And they asked me how long I have been in Abu Dhabi

I told them one month because by that time it was one month

They treated me for two days

Then the police came and removed me from the hospital

and took me to Dubai jail

I stayed there for one day because I was bleeding too much

and then the Abu Dhabi police came

and took me to the Department of the Police

I slept there for four days and I was still bleeding too much

They took me to the court

I told them all that happened

They sent me to the shelter

But the first shelter was not good

I found one lady, one Pakistan lady

She asked me what happened

She took care of me

She asked me if I wanted to eat or drink

She gave me a bed to rest in

I saw the others

They told me they would do everything they can for me

They accompanied me to the court until the case was over

Then they started to treat me

They took me to many hospitals

They took me to expensive hospitals

I was bleeding all that month

I came back

I slept when it was night

The bleeding never stopped

I called the supervisors

Then a doctor came and I fainted

She did her best and she cleaned me

She did not fear the blood

She took me to Sheikh Khalifa Hospital

They treated me very well there

I love that hospital

I was a victim in their country but they showed me love

I will never forget that hospital Sheikh Khalifa Hospital

Now I am good

As she said the sentences I repeated them and wrote word for word. (It has been edited here for clarity.) At the end, a weight was lifted from her, and there was a great sense of relief in the room.

"Ritha, would you like me to read this story to you?" I asked.

"No!" she said. "I know that story well. You take that story. That is for you."

"Can I share it with others?"

"Please do," she said. "I want to help others with that story."

We sat for a while, the kind doctor with us the whole time.

I left Ritha the journal and told her it was there for her if she felt like writing. She smiled. I also left with her a poem called "The Angel Who Lost His Wings," but I did not read it. Enough had been said by then and I could tell Ritha was tired.

I said goodbye and wished her a good trip home. It was hard to leave; there was so much shared. Before I left, I mentioned my work as a poetry therapist at a safe house. I also mentioned that I too have been abused when I was younger, and I understood the feelings. It felt right to share this with her.

I was allotted only one visit with Ritha, but I wanted to see her again. Would this be the right thing? Was it professional? When I talked to a friend who was very involved in social work, she told me I should go.

I had just bought two beautiful scarves for myself: one green and one pink. I was wearing the green one, and I decided to give the pink one to Ritha with a small booklet of poems I had put together for my workshops. After I called and got permission from the hospital, I gathered it all up and headed out.

Ritha seemed a bit brighter, and she was happy to be going home soon. I sat with her for a while and gave her the beautiful pink scarf. She put it on with a smile and said she would wear it on her trip home.

I took out the medicine—the packet of poems I had brought. There was one poem in particular I wanted to work from called "Windows."

"Do you feel like writing today?" I asked Ritha.

"Yes," she said.

"Why don't I read a poem first and then we will write?" I asked.

I turned to the poem, and she gently took the little booklet of poetry from me and started reading the poem. She read each word, each sentence in the most eloquent way, pausing to look at me throughout.

Windows

All I want is a window
A window of my very own

    All I want is a window
    A window to look out into the world
    A window to look deeply into the soul

All I want is a window
A window to sit in front of and dream
A window to sit in front of and create
A window to sit in front of and write

    All I want is a window
    A window open and wide to possibilities
    A window open and wide to hopes
    A window open wide to prospects
    A window open wide to opportunities

All I want is a window

A window framed by peace

A window fabricated by joy

A window bordered by freedom

A window surrounded by grace

A window constructed by love

    All I want is a window

    A window that will allow me to see many visions

    A window that will allow me to hear many voices

    A window that will allow me to taste many delicacies

    A window that will allow me to feel many touches

    A window that will allow me to smell many aromas

    A window that will allow me to imagine a new way of being in a new world

All I want is a window

A window through which I can leap

A window through which I can fly

A window through which I can soar

All I want is a window....

                                                            Trina-Leshay Johnson

When she finished she looked up, and then she repeated a few of the lines.

Ritha was a natural at poetry therapy. This is what we usually do at the end of a poem, mirror back lines.

I asked if she wanted to write from the prompt. She agreed, and I wrote as she spoke.

All I want is a window...

A window to take care of my family

A window to know God

A window to gain favor in my business

A window to be faithful to my son

A window to be strong in everything I do

A window to allow me to see my future

I asked her if she wanted me to read it back to her, and she said yes. I noticed there was a nurse in the room, and as I finished reading the poem, I explained to the nurse that this was a poem Ritha wrote. When I finished, both Ritha and the nurse smiled. I gave Ritha and the nurses some Persian sweets: pistachio baklava flavored with rose water, some saffron, and cardamom. She had her booklet from the day before, and we looked through it. She stopped at a poem, and I began to read it for her.

Silent Prayer

I walk toward you to find myself

I find the path to the river

I want to bow down and

feel my forehead in prayer

I want to watch myself

in the reflection of the lake

I pause

    I listen

        I breathe

            I hear the owl call my name

I feel the sun praise my name

Soul Spring

Child of God

I bow as I watch my shadow fall to the ground

There I find myself

and

I write in silence

Bahareh

"That is actually one of mine," I said.

She looked at me kindly, "I know," she said.

I was touched. "Do you want to write a poem together?" I asked.

Here is the poem Ritha and I wrote together:

We sit together in Peace and Silence as we write

We were talking of the problems we face in this world

We find this world is not easy

I find I am sitting in front of a mirror

One day I kept quiet

I wanted to get up on the balcony and fall down

because of the problems I got

I listened to my heart

My heart told me

Why do you do that

God still loves you

And your family still loves you

I thought it was an Angel

who is trying to defend me

I sat down and I started to cry

I asked my heart again

Why is it always me?

My heart told me it's not only you

But you have to believe in God

because many people want what you have received

but they cannot have it and they need help but no one can help them

So don't worry

Just pray for God

God will save

YOU

Ritha then had to get some x-rays done. I went down with her and waited. She told me to come in, and I talked to her during the x-ray. On our way back to the room, we passed the flower shop, and she said she wanted some.

I said, "A flower? Sure."

"No this one," she said. "The biggest one here."

"But you are leaving in a few hours."

"I want to take it with me in my suitcase, or I will carry it."

I thought she was kidding, but she was not. We settled on an arrangement of chocolates.

"Hopefully, your son will enjoy it as well," I said.

"No, I will keep it like this as decoration and a memory," she said.

We went to her room and talked for a while. I thanked her for our time together and reminded her of the simplicity of writing her feelings.

"Don't worry about me," she said. "I will go home, and the doctors will help me with their traditional medicine. I will send a picture to the hospital when I get nice and fat. I was so beautiful when I got here. I was 85 kilos!" (When I met her, she was skin and bones.) "Soon, I will be like that again," she said. I said goodbye, and one of her friends called her. I was happy she was on the phone as I left so she wouldn't be alone. I left with a heart full of love, hope, sorrow, but mostly full of beauty. I was grateful to see the effect of the medicine of words.

A Poem for Ritha

Ritha you came into my life to tell me something

I came into your life to hear something

You told me of the abuse and the blood

I heard the cries and saw the tears

You trusted my web of love

You gave to me without holding back

You told me of the sex work you did not choose

You told me of the dignity you had lost

You told me of the woman who brought you men

As you said "three men in one day to forced themselves on me me"

"I was bleeding" you said

The woman said, "I do not care"

I held your blood

I held your voice

Poetry Therapy with Ritha

I released your being

You gave me flight with your trust

I the healer

You the healer

We holding hands

No rubber gloves

Just trust and love

With this recognition of the truth of human trafficking

I see the world in a different light

Thank you for the voice

Thank you for the vision

Thank you for the trust

Mutual

Love

Tapping by the Sea

Abu Dhabi – April 2016

I was walking out by the sea one afternoon, not long ago, on the beach across the street from our house. I noticed a young lady and a slightly older one also walking along. I was attracted by their energy, but I simply looked and walked by.

On my way back, I saw the pair again.

"Hello," I said to the mother.

She looked at me, beaming. "I'm surprised there are still people who say a nice hello."

"I was attracted by the energy of you and your daughter," I explained. "You both looked so positive."

The back and forth continued, and I asked if I can walk with them for a while. As we walked, we shared some stories from our lives, about our children and such. She told me that her daughter had specifically asked for this walk on the beach, since she was a teacher and did not have much free time. I felt bad for interrupting their walk, but she assured me it was no problem. I noticed that she was holding both their phones in her hand and chuckled to myself.

I told her I do poetry therapy, and she was instantly intrigued and wanted to know more. She understood the concept in only a few moments and we did a quick poetry therapy session as we were walking. She was delighted and so was I.

The name of my newly found friend was Asefah. She was originally from Palestine. Asefah asked me if I knew about a therapy called Emotional Freedom Therapy, of EFT.

"No," I said.

"It is also known as tapping therapy," she explained, "one taps on nine different meridians of the body and this can make a difference in mood or an action that one is concentrated on. Do you want to try it?"

I am a sucker for things like that, so I said yes.

"Is there anything you want to work on," she asked, "for example, are you scared of anything?"

"Yes, driving on the freeway," I said. I told her about how I was too scared to go to the new mall that opened 20 minutes away because I did not want to drive on the freeway. I also could never go to Dubai if I was driving; lots of times I would have to take a taxi.

"From one to ten, how scared or anxious does this make you?"

"Ten."

We started tapping the way she instructed me to: first on the side of the hand expressing the emotion, and then saying how I accept and love myself regardless of the anxiety. Then by the eyebrow, the temple, then below the eye, under the nose, on the chin, on the chest close to neck, under the arm, and on top of the head. It was a lot of tapping. We did this several times together then she asked me again how scared I was from one to ten.

"Six," I said. We continued to talk about EFT. "I'll drive to the mall and let you know how it goes."

We walked back and found Dana her daughter sitting peacefully. "Sorry to take your mom away," I told her. She smiled. It seemed like she was at peace without her phone, with nothing to distract her from enjoying the beach. We all walked back toward our homes together, since they live only a block away from me.

Two days later, I really did drive to the mall. I also took a selfie while at the new mall and sent it to Asefah. The day after that I drove myself to Dubai. To this day, I still can't believe how well the tapping therapy worked. Now, when I sit in the car, I tap for a few minutes before getting on the road.

We have not seen each other since that day at the beach, but continue to send each other messages. I always wanted to stop by with a basket of flowers to thank her for her time, for her tapping, and for her smile.

So far, I've only managed to send the flowers on Whatsapp: a few beautiful pictures, but the real ones would be so much nicer. I need to do that before I leave this home by the beach that has brought me such good friends and travel companions by the sea.

Who Would Have Thought Tweeting Could Lead to Lida

Dubai – 2011

My dear friend Farzad and I were riding in the car together from Abu Dhabi to Dubai to go hear a TEDx talk. He had been wanting to teach me about Twitter for a while, so he took the opportunity during the long car ride. I was ready to learn.

He told me all about hashtags, and I tried my hand at a tweet or two. Only a few minutes later, someone had retweeted me! What a fantastically interesting thing! Excitedly, I showed Farzad.

We went to the TEDx conference and enjoyed the presentations. Eager to capitalize on my recent technological discovery, I was busy Tweeting about the event the whole time. Apparently, I was quite good at describing a TED talk in 140 characters. One person, by the name of Lida, retweeted me a couple of times. I asked her if she was at the talk in a message. She must have laughed at my inexpertise in the Twitterverse. She was at home watching online, unable to attend the actual program.

From then on, Lida and I kept in contact by e-mail. Then, Lida came to one of my poetry recitals in Dubai. I was so happy, and in a way surprised, to see her there.

A while later, we set a date to meet up so that she could teach me more about Twitter and technology. We talked and talked, but not much about technology since, by that time, I had forgotten most of my online passwords. We decided to learn about technology the next time we met up. I never did learn much though, so not much has changed in that department to this day.

What has changed though, is that now Lida and I are real friends. She has become part of my journey in life, and I have become part of hers. We talk to each other in far more than just 140 characters. We have been there for each other for gallery openings and recitals. At times, she has come to support me, and at times, I have gone to support her. The fantastic thing is that even when we are not present with each other, we know that we are there. We also share the passion of the here and now with each other. She writes about the beauty of living with mindfulness on her blog, here2here, and her art, iphonography, is all about capturing the moment. How grateful I am for that day and for my friend, Farzad, who taught me how to Tweet. Even though I do not Tweet too much these days, I will always cherish the fact that I found such a beautiful travel companion in just 140 characters.

Vera: Meetings in the Sky

The Flight from San Francisco to Washington, DC – 2002

After visiting family in California, on a flight home to Washington, DC, I sat in one of the four middle seats. There was one empty space and a lady sitting to my left. I felt so much like talking to someone. I looked at her; she had her music or something in her ear and didn't quite seem like she was in the talking mood.

I caught her eye, and she smiled at me. We started talking, and she told me her name was Vera.

"Vera," I said. "I need company... I am feeling sad..."

It is so freeing to be able to tell someone that: "I am sad, I need someone to talk to".

That is the beauty of airplanes, isn't it? You meet someone, you share some time and some words, and then you go about your life and they goes about theirs. This is the beauty of meetings in flight.

After talking and sharing stories for a while, I opened my purse and took out the bag of snacks my mother had prepared for me. There were some nuts and fruits and other simple things. I extended my hand and asked Vera if she would like some.

"No," she said. I thought maybe she might be allergic to nuts, so I offered the fruit.

"I cannot eat," she said.

Surprised, I asked, "What do you mean?"

"I have a condition," she said. "My body does not accept food. Every time I eat, I am in terrible pain for quite a long time. I have basically stopped eating, and I get my calories in the form of liquid now. I also take a lot of capsules and pills, some with nutritional value and others with medicinal value."

I found out that her work was to help develop programs for the starving. How incredible to be in her position and to still find the drive to help others. The true lessons and miracles of life.

When she told me she was related to Eleanor Roosevelt (mentioned casually as if she did not want to show off), I said, "Oh, I see how you are just as determined and how you will make such a big difference in the world as well."

When we got off the plane, I felt much lighter having shared the time we had together. We exchanged e-mails and phone numbers, and even now, after 15 years, we keep in touch. At the time, she lived on the West Coast of America and I lived on the East Coast of America, but I guess distance is not really an issue when hearts and souls connect.

She was coming to Washington, DC with her son for a family reunion.

When she was in town, we invited them over for a visit. My girls were about the same age as her son, Mark. My mother was also visiting from California, so we all sat around the table. I had insisted not to gather for dinner so that Vera would not have to sit and watch us eat, but she assured me that she was comfortable.

We all sat together and shared soul food. Vera's smile takes over the entire world, just as it had taken over my heart that night in the sky.

Mark also captured all of our hearts. It is as if we were related from long ago somehow, and maybe we were. Maybe we are.

I saw Vera a couple more times when I was in California visiting family, and from then on, it has been small hellos on the internet. The connection that was made all those years ago is so deep that I often turn to her Facebook page specifically to see her smile.

I have never seen such a smile in my life: a smile of a woman who is not hungry for anything in life. A smile of a soul that feeds the world with her being.

How fortunate I am to have been there that night, sad and reaching out to such an open heart and open soul. Blessings are always everywhere.

Recently, I looked her up to see what she is up to. I Googled her, and found that besides being a researcher and professor, she is Deputy Director at one of the largest charitable foundations in the world. Most importantly for me, though, she will always be the open heart I reached out to far above the ground in the sky. A human being touching hearts.

Meeting the Poet Who Dared to Bungee Jump
Abu Dhabi – 2012

A few years after arriving in Abu Dhabi, some time after poetry first made a home in my heart, and after several solo poetry recitals, the path made it possible for a night of poetry and music that would involve the entire community.

With my involvement at the safe houses, labor camps, schools, and universities, there was a wide range of talent to bring onto the stage. We called it "Speak Abu Dhabi". We were getting ready for the May event and we were still looking for a couple more poets. We thought it would be great to feature an artist from the Emirates.

We spread the word, and one day someone called me and said she had found an Emirati poetess. I was delighted and eagerly asked how I could contact her.

"Oh, but she is handicapped," the lady said. I did not know why she found it necessary to say "but", as if being handicapped would be a problem for me.

"Great," I said, "as long as she is willing to talk about the program."

That was the beginning of a magical friendship. Hada is indeed physically challenged and has been since she was young. Her voice is soothing, and her poetry is like music for the soul. However, she is so much more than a poet: she is an advocate for human rights and an advocate for the voice of women. She talks about how despite all the odds that were against her, she went to America to a university in Arizona to study. She made it possible all by her own will, all by her own vision.

She told me me that on a day while she was in Arizona, there was an opportunity for a bungee jumping expedition. She went along with the other students and insisted that she wanted to do it. Everyone around her said no, but her teacher said if she felt like it and wanted to, then why not. They had to make adjustments to the security belt, but Hada did it! She says from that moment on, she knew she could do anything in the world.

While preparing for Speak Abu Dhabi, she was being courted by a young man. It was hard because he was from a different culture, but she listened to her heart, and she got married a few days after Speak Abu Dhabi. A year and half later, while we were getting ready for the second Speak Abu Dhabi, Hada was pregnant, against all odds.

I see her smile and I learn. I see her heart and I glow with happiness. How fortunate I am to have crossed paths with someone so brave, someone so real.

Filipino Safe House
Abu Dhabi – 2009

I did not know my way around town very well yet, so we met in the parking lot of a church, which I still had trouble finding. I found the petite Patricia in a big SUV. Her accomplishments, however, were far from petite. She was a family lawyer and judge in the US and here had turned her attention to social work and her own family.

"You know, you could do your own thing with the ladies at the safe house," said Patricia, as we sat in her car on the way to the Filipino Safe House. "Some people do help with painting or jewelry making. I teach yoga, for example."

"I don't really know what I could do," I replied, "I'll just sit and watch you today."

We arrived, and I walked in to find a room with more than 30 ladies. The house consisted of about five rooms, each one with three or four bunk beds. One could see the ladies storing their clothes under the bed or hanging from the bed.

Patricia went up to the front while I stayed in back. I noticed a stack of Bibles and reached for one and started reading. I can't say I was praying, but I know I was deep in my own presence. I was only vaguely aware of Patricia and the ladies doing yoga.

Time flew by, and before I knew it, we were talking to the ladies and getting back into the car. When I got back home, the Safe House, the home of those ladies, clung to my thoughts.

Only a few days later, Patricia called me to ask if I could take her spot at the safe house the following week, seeing as she could not make it. She knew how disappointed the ladies got when one of the volunteers does not show up; they look forward to it all week.

Next week came around, and I managed to find the place on my own, getting only slightly lost. I sat in the car for a few moments, praying, with no Bible or other holy book this time. I prayed that I would be guided to do what I am supposed to do, if there was a reason for it. There were some apples in my car that I brought with me, as well as a knife that was gifted to me by a dear friend's daughter.

I put the things in my bag and went in. Right away, I was greeted with love and warmth. I automatically felt at home. When I was asked what I do, I simply told them that I was a storyteller. This time we sat downstairs in the main lobby; a big circle of sisters.

It's always strange to open the circle by introducing ourselves, so I decided to start with a story so that we could develop trust in the space. The story, thankfully, needs apples. I called it the apple story. A teacher told it to me years ago, and I have since told adaptations of it hundreds of times.

 "We, the group, have been told that there is a treasure in the jungle, and we must go on a search." I explained. "There, we meet an old lady, who points into the depths of the jungle and tells us to find the treasure. When we return, we each have an apple in hand. The old lady asks us what we found, and each of us responds with something different, for example, the sun, the moon, the trees, a new friendship, and so on. The old lady says, "Yes, all those are treasures, but the real treasure is right here." I took the knife, and cut my apple in half from side to side, not the usual way from the stem. When we looked into the middle of the apple, the seeds made a star.

Pretending to be the old lady, I said, "We each have a shining star within us. We each have something that is so special, that no one else has and no one can take away. We can always reach in for that star to guide us."

From there, I did not have to do anything but listen. The ladies talked about their shining stars and what made them all special. They started to talk about their families and how much they missed them. They all talked about the situations they had found themselves in. The ladies had been in some situations that are truly hard to mention.

From that moment, I became known as the storyteller and went each week. In reality, I went to hear their stories: to let their stories have a place to breathe and just *be*. I was so thankful that Patricia took me there in the first place and gave me the space to find so many shining stars, who are all still in my heart. Many of the ladies became Facebook friends, and from time to time write to me and ask how I am doing. Some have found other jobs here, while others have moved back home to their families.

May we all, wherever we are, feel safely at home and appreciate our own shining stars, as well as the light within others.

The Power of Art and Poetry: Meeting Larry

London – December 2013

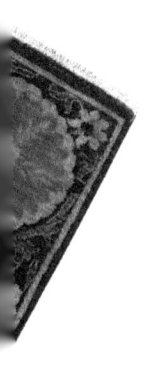

While on a walk in London with my family, my husband noticed a painting in the window of a gallery.

"Oh, what a nice painting," he said casually, and kept on walking. I stopped and looked. The painting was powerful, despite its small size. It was about the size of a piece of paper, but it was so vibrant: the yellows and oranges, the hues of light, beauty shining though the small tree and small person in the painting. I told my husband and my daughters to go on walking without me, and I stepped inside the shop.

I felt like I had stepped inside of a treasure box. I felt like Alice falling into the rabbit hole and finding wonderland.

"Hello," I said to the gentleman behind the table as I walked in, "is this your art?" He was talking to another lady. I did not want to interrupt, but I also wanted to learn more.

The gentleman, who I would later discover was named Larry, got up and walked over to me. He was tall and well dressed. "Yes, this is all my art," he said, "I have been painting for thirty years." I felt an incredible connection, as if we had been brother and sister in another time and had finally been brought together. There was a gentle understanding that we saw each other.

Larry started to tell me his story in detail. I was drawn in instantly. He was originally from Nigeria, but born in the UK, and had lived in Nigeria for many years. At age 19, he moved to London with his family. Larry came from a family of comfortable means, and his father wanted him to study law. Knowing that his true passion was art, Larry refused, and his father told him he would have to be on his own. Eventually, he ended up on the streets: homeless, addicted to drugs, and on the verge of giving up.

A chance encounter with an Irish man, who had served 20 years in prison, gave Larry a change in perspective. The man encouraged Larry to use his gift, his artistic talent, to help those who were in prison. When Larry got there and started teaching, he could suddenly see himself as one of the prisoners. From that moment, he decided to take initiative and change his life. He has now helped over 5,000 ex-offenders and inmates learn skills. He also works with victims of crime, schools, colleges, and businesses. Hearing his stories about all the lives he has touched in the past thirty years was truly amazing.

His story was a touching one, as there were both Light and Dark moments, but it was the Light that shone through his words and the paintings that surrounded us while we talked. The lady, a mentee of Larry's who was sitting at the table when I walked in, came over to us.

"You know what," she said, "I had always seen despair in these paintings but now I begin to see the true light and hope."

Larry walked over to the window of his gallery and pulled out the painting my husband had noticed and I had inquired about. He flipped it over and started writing on the back:

My dearest sister,
Bahareh Amidi,

I am so blessed to have reconnected with you.
This is the Lord's doing, it is marvelous in my eyes.

Lots of love
Larry
December 31st 2013
God bless

He handed me the beautiful painting, called "The Tree of Life". I accepted humbly, and I knew I was touched by Light at that moment. There is always a reason for every meeting, every breath.

The painting hangs in our home and fills my heart and soul with the gift of Life and Light. Words cannot express the gratitude I feel, but they can express some of the emotions I had during that experience. Later that evening I wrote to Larry:

Colors of Light

A deep breath in and I enter a prison cell

I was just walking around with my family

But the divine had other plans for me on this last day of the year

The cell I walked into was made of color and Light

There I met a brother, one I knew from another time

He told me the story of how he has helped so many

in the cell

"The Cell Empty of Light"

I found myself intrigued...

I was taken to a place and time before

When I was walking on the street

When I met a man with color on his hands

but no home to sleep

A man of honor and dignity

This man I know

The Power of Art and Poetry: Meeting Larry

My brother who has found his wings in flight

My brother who gives others wings to fly

The dear artist who has roots deep into mother earth

The brother whose vision is bringing art to all

I am humbled by the connections of Light

Today I feel the blessing of the "Tree of Life" on my path

Today I have seen the "Walking To the Light"

I thank thee for this day

for this message for the messenger in disguise

I thank thee for the beauty for the creations and the creator

A breath out and I know that I have been shown Light

Happy New Year

Bahareh

Larry and I have been in contact since that day. His story has touched so many lives and has had a ripple effect in my universe. I know that we will host Larry sometime in the future in Abu Dhabi. His art needs to find a place in our homes and hearts so that his story can inspire us to give more of ourselves in order to touch the lives of others.

Larry has expressed that when he comes to Abu Dhabi, or when he visits anywhere else in the world, 20 percent of his art sales will go to a local cause. I have started dreaming of the lives and hearts he will touch when he comes, the places we will visit: the schools, universities, prisons, hospitals, labor camps and so much more. Don't worry, I will take him to the Grand Mosque and all the sites, for his heart will glow with the beauty of what man has made out of a desert land.

During the time I was in Larry's gallery, my family was having tea, and when I came back, painting in hand, my husband was stunned by its beauty, but more so by the gesture. He went back to meet Larry and to thank him personally.

Meeting Neshat - The Reality of Words Touching Hearts

Abu Dhabi - 2011

I woke up to a Facebook message from a lovely lady who had seen me on a TV program in Dubai. She said that when she heard me speak she knew she had to find me.

Her name was Neshat, and she wrote to me saying she could not believe it when she saw this program about me and my poetry. I had been on a news program as a follow up to one of my recitals, and they had aired a couple of my poems.

We exchanged phone numbers, and we got to talking on a regular basis. She told me that she had been in a very bad place in her life, and my poetry was just what she needed to hear. She started to read my poetry in Farsi on my website called NedaazNoor which when translated means "Message from Light". She says she had been brought out of darkness into light.

I went to Dubai, where she lived, to meet her. It seemed as if we had known each other for years, and we had, I am sure. We've known each other for years and years in the core of our lives and beings.

Neshat came to a few of my recitals, and it was such a joy to see her heart, full of light, in the audience. The lightness carried on past my recitals, and she shared the joys of becoming a grandmother, as well as her journey through life.

Nowadays, I am in touch with her from time to time on Facebook, and we call each other on birthdays and such. It has been a pleasure to celebrate and be a part of each other's life's milestones.

A Moment on the Sidewalk

Menlo Park, California – March 2013

I was passing by and saw a lady sitting on the ground, almost in the middle of the sidewalk. She was holding a book. I leaned over as I was passing by and noticed it was a poetry book.

"Oh, you are reading poetry," I said.

I sat down next to her, mirroring her cross-legged position. We started talking for a few minutes. She was waiting for her shuttle to pick her up. She said she had been coming there for years to meet her therapist.

She pointed across the street and said, "Do you see those roses across the street? I have been admiring them for years, I want to have one to paint."

I asked her if I could go and get one for her with the permission of the owner, she replied, "No when it is time, it will be."

"Do you always stop to talk to people?" she asked me.

I said, "Your energy drew me in and I wanted to talk to you"

"That is interesting because people usually think I am a homeless person as I sit and read on the sidewalk."

We sat for a few minutes sharing this sacred space of no words, but feelings. From one person to another, two travel companions on a journey sharing a moment on the side walk along with talk of poetry and art and roses.

In a moment, her shuttle arrived. I gave her a hand up after I got up from the space I had sat in next to her. I hugged her, and she hugged me back really hard. She said she really needed this love.

I could feel her love, and I could also feel how she needed it. At that time, we said each of us would read a poem for the other that night. As she got onto her shuttle, we waved goodbye and sent air kisses.

I will never forget the poetry of a rose and an encounter on a sidewalk and a tale of two strangers meeting hearts.

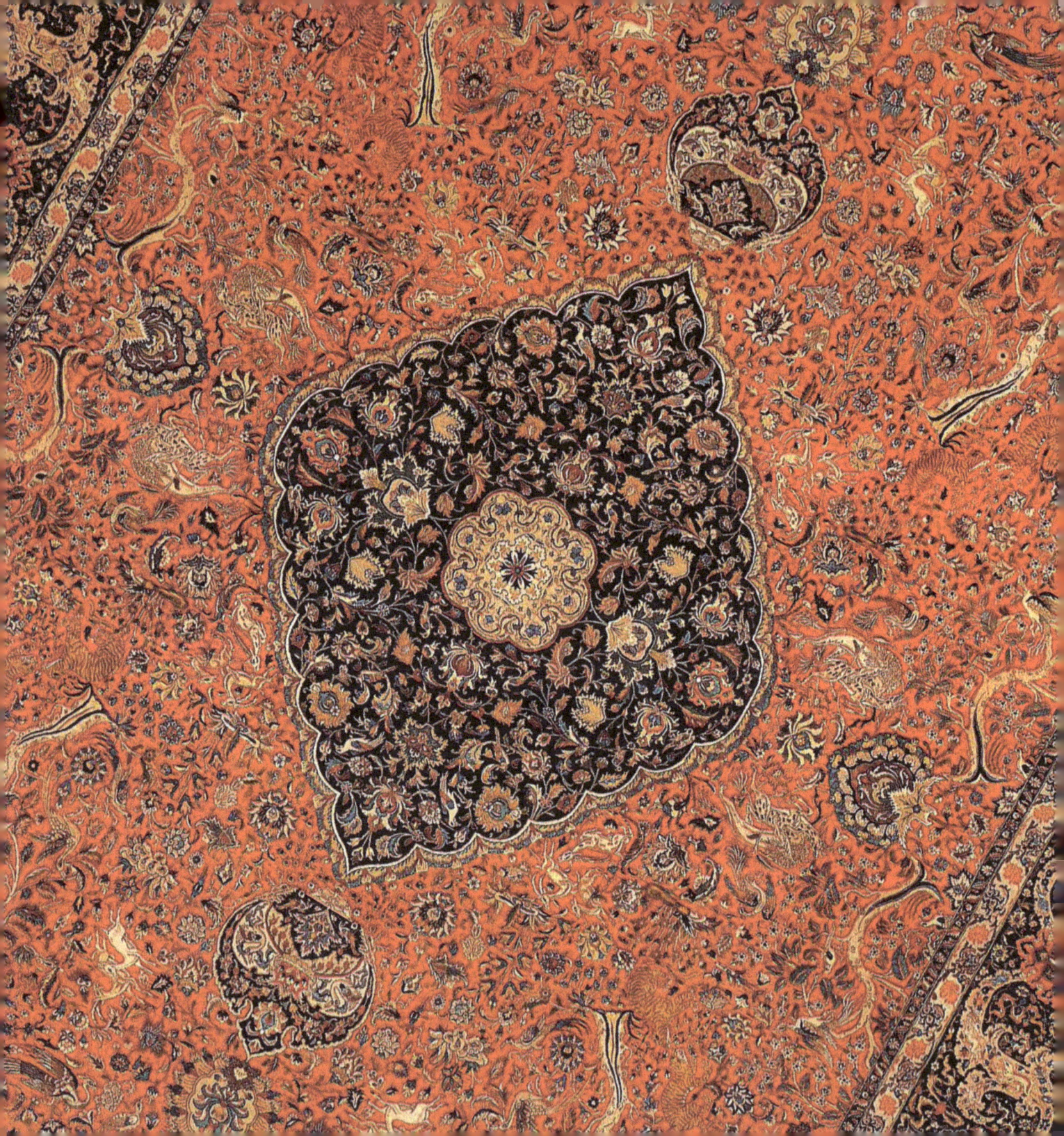

The Smile Behind the Search

Abu Dhabi – September 2015

"I will let Dr. A know that you are here," said the lady at the front desk of the long term care center. I was there to talk to the doctor about poetry therapy.

"No, please," I replied. "Do not let him know. I am here early and I would like to sit and read something before I meet him."

I went into the waiting room and was stopped in my tracks by the smile I saw. A beautiful lady was sitting, waiting, with such a divine, soulful presence. I sat on the other side of the waiting room. She never looked up, but somehow I was drawn to look at her. She had stunning eyes and a great color lipstick of pink that matched her charming scarf. I did not walk up to her and say hello as I usually do when I encounter an interesting person.

It was time for my meeting, so I left. It was wonderful to see the doctor and his associate and share some time talking about poetry therapy and how it could help those in the care facility. I mentioned how it can be instrumental for the nurses and doctors, and even the families of the patients.

As I left the meeting room and came back into the hallway, I noticed that the beautiful lady was still there. I had asked the receptionist to call a cab for me, but then I decided to tell her to wait. I remembered a dear friend that lived close by who I might be able to visit. I called, but she was not available.

As I returned to the waiting area, I finally said hello to the lady with the lovely smile.

"Are you still waiting?"

"Yes," she said. She had come without an appointment and was inquiring about a job.

"How lucky they would be to have you," I said, "with such a smile and such great energy."

"Wow, I needed that reinforcement," she replied. I hugged her and said she knew how wonderful she was and that she must just remember the gifts she brought. Her name was Maryam.

Someone came to the waiting room to call her in.

"Good luck!" I said as she was leaving, "any place would be lucky to have you!" She went off and I sat back down to think of anyone else I could call to go and see in the area.

As I got up to go and ask the receptionist to call a cab for me, Maryam walked toward the desk to get her ID and return the guest pass. I asked her where she was headed.

"Anywhere you tell me, I will take you," she said kindly.

"No, really," I insisted, "tell me where you are going."

"I am going to Al Salam street."

This was not too far from where I lived, so I asked if she would give me a ride.

"Happily." she said.

"So I will not call you a taxi," said the receptionist, smiling.

Maryam said she would go start the car so it wouldn't be too hot, but I told her it would be fine and we could go together.

"I have a humble car," she said, shyly.

"It seems it got you here!", I replied with a smile.

We talked about life and work and family and all. She is originally from Somaliland and said her father had come to the UAE when he was sixteen years old. In those days, he would walk from Dubai to Abu Dhabi, since only the Sheikh had a car at that time. She said that someone had offered her father an Emirati passport for 500 dirhams, which was a lot of money back then. Now, it is something no amount of money can buy. Maryam's children are the third generation to live here, but they still cannot hold an Emirati passport.

Maryam was the third child of eight, and she studied to be a dentist and had finished school and started the training process when they told her that the training was only for UAE locals. Even though she was born here, the government officials told her to go back to her country and do the training. There is no dentistry training in Somaliland, so she changed her career path and became a case supervisor and coordinator.

"Do you have time for lunch?" I asked her. She said yes. "What is your favorite restaurant?"

"Indian Palace," she replied.

"Great! Let's go!"

After finally winning the lengthy argument about who would treat who to lunch, we made our way there. It was a beautiful restaurant, and I could not believe that after all these years living here I had never been. On Maryam's suggestion, we went upstairs to one of the private family rooms. I had always wondered why people would choose these rooms, since I like sitting with and seeing people I don't know, but Maryam said you could be more at ease, especially if you were covered and wanted to loosen your scarf. That day the private setting was perfect. She ordered some food, and a great mango juice.

We talked and shared soul food and the spices of life. We also looked at a small poetry therapy book I had recently written. I mentioned to her how poetry therapy works, and how it could heal.

We wrote together and shared our words and voices.

To remember the moment and our day together, we took a selfie. I shared the picture with my family, and I am sure she shared it with her family as well. The reality is that no amount of words or pictures can capture the feelings and the essence of what was shared. Nonetheless, I like coming back to this story just to get a flavor of the smile, the meeting, and the spices shared at Indian Palace and the Palace of Life.

Car Wash Encounter

Abu Dhabi – Fall 2015

It was another wonderful day. I had gone to a psychiatry conference about Transcranial Magnetic Stimulation, which I enjoyed. There were still a couple of hours left before I had to go and pick up my youngest daughter from soccer practice at school so I decided to go get my car washed.

As I was sitting on a bench by where the car would be cleaned, I saw a woman in front of me leaning out of a car, a very fancy Range Rover with dark windows. There was another lady sitting in the passenger seat next to her. The woman in the driver's seat was shouting at the Filipino manager and an Indian man who vacuums inside the cars. As the one-sided conversation got louder, I overheard something about soiling. I could not help but feel like I had to walk up to this situation.

"I am so sorry to intrude," I said, "but I could not help but overhear your conversation, and since something like this happened to me before, I thought I would share my experience with you."

The lady hanging out of the car, with a half-worn head scarf and a face full of makeup, leaned further out and said, "Oh, so they did this to you too?"

"Well, once I was getting out of the car here, and dropped my scarf as I was getting out, and it got a bit soiled," I responded. "It was an accident, just an accident, it happens."

"Well, he did this," the lady said, as she pointed at the man, "not me."

I gently pointed out that the point was that it was an accident, and it could happen to anyone, at any time. The arguing went back and forth for a while, until finally, the driver of the fancy car, who was actually an Abu Dhabi local, got out of the car, with her incredibly high-heeled shoes, kilos of makeup, and strong perfume, and waved a badge in front of the eyes of the manager and the worker, who was shaking in fear.

"You know where I work?" the woman said, "I could report you! And deport you!"

I, trying to calm the situation, offered to clean it, and was brought a bucket of fresh water by

the shivering man. I had an article of clothing in my car that was on route to the dry cleaner's, and so, using it as a rag, I dipped it in the water and onto the soiled piece of clothing, but to no avail. I mentioned how this would come out at a dry cleaner's in no time at all.

"The man can take it himself," she said.

"Thank you," I said, half bowing and grateful that she had reached a calmer conclusion.

The men smiled, and I could sense the relief. Finally, the ladies in the car decided to take the scarf, get it cleaned, and bring the bill back, and everyone was relatively happy. After the ladies walked towards their fancy car, I offered the manager some money to cover the dry cleaning bill, but he refused. Next, I walked over to the lady's car to give her my card.

"Let us get together for tea sometime," I offered. Instead, they invited me to lunch .

"I've already had lunch," I replied, "but would love to join you for tea."

I followed them to their local hangout near the

mall. We sat outside at their regular table. The waiter immediately brought them their shisha.

"Do you want one?" they asked me.

I do not smoke, but I said why not, and got one anyway. They ordered lunch (a whole sea food platter and soup), and I got a mint tea. We got to talking, and each of their stories was fascinating: full of color and in some ways full of darkness. No wonder they raised their voices at that poor man at the carwash, I thought.

The local lady had been married twice, and had not yet been able to get pregnant. She had been abused when she was younger. She was well off, but not well. She lived a life of comfort with a nice car and probably a nice home and all, but in reality her being was not comfortable. The other lady, I found out, was from England and used to live there in Abu Dhabi. Her family moved back to England, but she wanted to stay in Abu Dhabi and had converted to Islam, making her family unhappy. Now, the English woman was the best friend of the Emirati lady, and she had even chosen a name similar to hers. The young British lady had no visa and was worried she would have to leave.

We talked, and then they asked about what I did. I told them I was a poetry therapist and asked them if they wanted to write. They both said yes, so we wrote and shared what we had written. Quickly, they both became emotional, and were worried that their makeup would be ruined. In just a couple of lines, a lot came out. I wanted to talk more deeply about the writings, but they did not, so I let it be.

We talked a bit longer, and they finished their lunch.

"How fortunate we are to share such a time," I mentioned casually, "our lunch would equal half of the car wash man's monthly salary." I know they heard me, but they did not react.

Slowly, I headed out, they both thanked me and said something about my kindness in the car wash situation, and I thanked them too. I felt I needed them to know I was grateful for them letting me walk into the situation, and for this newly found friendship.

We went on our separate ways. The British girl wrote to me a couple times on Whatsapp, first to say hello and if I wanted to join them for lunch again, then another time saying that her visa was giving her trouble, and then a while after that from England, saying she had gone back because she had no visa, no insurance, and a heart problem that needed medical attention.

I have often wondered if they ever went back to the car wash; if they went with the bill, or to apologize. I guess we all do what we need to do. I did what I needed to do when I was at the carwash and that was to stop the verbal abuse against the blameless car wash man.

May we all find it in our hearts to make another heart happy.

Shafana and the Prayer Beads

Abu Dhabi Airport – February 2013

——————— When I heard my mother was not feeling well, I decided to catch the next flight out to be with her in San Francisco.

The flight was delayed, so there was lots of waiting around. I went to the washroom and noticed a small prayer room off to the side. I decided to go sit and pray and be with my own thoughts.

After a while, I opened my eyes and in front of me were the most beautiful, clear, aqua blue prayer beads. In awe, I picked them up, and went outside and brought them to the lady who keeps the area clean. I asked her if I could keep the beads and that my mother was very sick and I needed her prayers.

"I am sure that the beads are for you," she said kindly.

We hugged, kissed, and exchanged names and numbers. Her name was Shafana and she was from Uganda: a beautiful lady inside and out. I found out that she had left her children behind and come to Abu Dhabi in hopes of providing a better life for them. She had been working in this washroom for over a year.

Off I went with my beautiful, soulful beads. I loved having them with me. They kept me company, but I thought it was really Shafana who was keeping me company the whole time.

I arrived in California, and Mother was not well. During the month and a half I stayed with her, Shafana would message me from time to time to ask how mother was doing. I knew that her prayers were with us, and I felt her soul and her blessings.

Slowly, Mother got better, Alhamdulillah (thank God). I returned home, but I still talked to Shafana.

The next time I saw her was when I was traveling with my daughters, this time a summer visit to see my family. I was a bit shy going to say hello to her because this was the second time in four months that I was traveling to see my mother, while Shafana had to wait two years to go and see her family. But shyness aside, I had to go and see her.

There she was once again. We hugged, kissed, shared some stories, and then I was off again. This time she took some white prayer beads out of her bag and gave them to me.

When I came back from the US, Shafana and I met outside of the airport. We spent a whole day together going around Abu Dhabi. It was hard for me to believe that after more than a year of living there, she had not been to the Grand Mosque, especially as a practicing Muslim. She said she had not yet had the opportunity. It was wonderful that we could share that together. We went and saw all the sights: from the nice views from atop the Emirates Palace Hotel to the beach to soak our feet in the salt water.

We continue to be in contact on a weekly basis and have become soul sisters. I know that we will continue to shed light on each other's lives for years to come.

Gratitude for the prayers, for the beads, and for the beauty from within.

Pigeon Mail: Express Delivery
Poetry Therapy across Continents – 2013 - 2014

November 26, 2013

Dear Bahareh,

I hope this email finds you well. I will introduce 'One Word' to my Master 1 Psychology students tomorrow as our Poetry Therapy sequel, and I am writing to plant a seed... Would you consider speaking to us if you were on a trip to France? Thank you in advance for your kind consideration and thank you for inspiring me.

Kindly,

A

November 26, 2013

Dearest A,

Hello, what an absolute delight to receive your message, your call. I take this as a gift, a gift and a reminder. I am honored to know that these words have touched your heart and soul, and I am honored that you are sharing it with your class.

This poem "Stop Me from Jumping over the Bridge of Life with ONE WORD", is actually a poem that is over one hundred verses long. We chose a few of those verses to make the video. Truly, until the very last moment, I was not sure what the word would be.

As you know, poetry is a gift to me.... a gift to remind me of how beautiful words are and how they can help an individual to express one's feelings. I believe that writing is the first step of healing and that it is when poetry is read and shared that the real healing begins to happen. Giving words a voice is so powerful.

I am touched by your invitation, and would absolutely love to come to talk with your class, I am not sure when that could be. I will be in London for the holidays, but I am afraid at that time your University will also be on break.

I have never done this, but as I read your email, an idea came into my mind.... I will just share it with you. I can certainly come for a visit to your classroom via Skype. We could spend some time talking about poetry therapy and even do a short five to seven minute writing together, just for everyone to get a sense of the magic of poetry therapy in action. I could send you a selection of three poems before we meet, and we might work with one of the poems. Again, this is just an idea that popped into my head and I thought I would share with you.

May I ask how you learned about my work? And how about Poetry Therapy, when did you become familiar with this gift. Please send my regards to your students. From me to you.... Gratitude.

Truly and always

In Light,

Bahareh

November 28, 2013

Dearest Bahareh,

I hope this message finds you very well. I am honored and excited about your prompt enthusiastic reply. I have shared with the students (who are equally excited) and must run your 'seed' through our administration to make sure we can begin growing our 'garden'.

As the semester is fast coming to its close, life on campus is rather busy and it might take me a little time to get back to you thoroughly. I thank you in advance for your patience and wish you a safe trip to Europe.

Sincerely,

A

November 29, 2013

Dearest A,

Hello, and thank you for writing back with such warmth. I am happy that you and the students are open to this idea, I am sure the details will work out in time. There is no hurry at all, I am here any time all the time.

B

February 17, 2014

Dear Bahareh,

I hope this email finds you well and that you had a smooth transition into the New Year. It seems that a Skype conference will not be possible on our campus for security reasons. Hence, I have thought hard as to make our seed flourish in the spring and here is what I'd like to suggest:

The students of the Department of Psychology, who I teach English to, have launched a Newspaper in which and English feature exists. If you agree, I'd like to gather student questions to you, organize a phone call or Skype from a non-campus location in order for a small group of student-journalists to interview you, edit the interview and submit it to the paper for publication this Spring Semester.

Would this idea suit you? I very much look forward to hearing from you.

Kindest regards,

A

February 18, 2014

Dearest A,

Hello, yes the transition to the New Year has been wonderful. I have just returned from my courses at The Institute for Poetic Medicine in California, I am charged and recharged with all the wonders of poetry and poetry as healer. I completely understand that some universities have their own rules and regulations. I think it is a fine idea you have, truly anything that you think will work will be wonderful for me.

Your passion and desire to bring this idea of Poetry Therapy to your students touches me so deeply, I wish I could just fly over and spend a couple of sessions in your class, just to be with you and your students and then if questions arose to answer them.... for now though I suggest we go with your suggestion.

Best and Always

In Light,

Bahareh

March 31, 2014

Dear Bahareh,

I hope this email finds you well and healthful.

The students have turned in their questions to me and I am writing to ask if you would be available either on the 2nd or 3rd week of April to interview. As we're not allowed to use Skype on campus for security reasons, the student journalists will come to my home.

Would either Friday at 7:00pm (9:00pm in Dubai) work? I look forward to hearing from and wish you a nice week.

Kindest regards,

A

April 1, 2014

Dearest A,

Hello, happy Spring to you, I hope that your life is filled with blossoms in the months to come. I am in awe of your perseverance, and I am honored that you will make such arrangements. I am in the U.S. and return around the 10th of April, so I would say that April 18th, which is the third week would be ideal at nine pm.

Please let me know how much time we will have together, I will be very flexible and in no hurry to go anywhere. I am asking because I find it would be fantastic to give the students a short, very short capsule talk on poetry as healer and then have them ask questions, or first ask and then i talk. It will also be great time for us to write together, even if it is for 3 to 5 minutes, they can really experience the magic of poetry therapy.

Touched by your kindness and really soooooo excited to meet you and your wonderful students.

Truly and Always

In Light,

Bahareh

April 3, 2014

Dear Bahareh,

Thank you for your speed-of-light response. We were inspired by you and are thrilled at the opportunity you are giving us to interview you...

It took me a little longer than expected to coordinate with the three student-journalists who will interview you and I would like to know if you could rather meet up on Monday, April 14th at 5:00pm in Metz/7:00pm in Dubai as opposed to the originally suggested Friday evening option.

Our questions are ready. Would you like a copy now or do you prefer to be surprised during our live-chat?

The students and I would genuinely enjoy the format you suggested (talk, interview, writing) and I believe an hour and a half will be sufficient for this workshop. What do you think? We can obviously shorten if need be on your end. As a single mom conducting the interview from my home, my son will also be in the audience!

I wish you a brilliant night and look forward as always to reading you.

Kindest regards,

A

April 26, 2014

Dearest A,

Hello, how are you? And your wonderful students. It was such a pleasure meeting you all on Skype call, really fantastic. The entire experience was something I enjoyed so much. I just got back to UAE and have been going through my emails and some work. I know that your students had some additional questions, I would be happy to answer those. Please feel free to send them to me.

Also, if there is anything else I can add to our conversation to make the experience with poetry therapy more complete please let me know. Again, thank you for your time, for your diligence in making it all happen.

Truly yours,

In Light,

Bahareh

Also, thank you opening up in your writing, especially since it was in front of your students. It takes a special person to do that. I think it also takes a special space we all created together, a space of respecting each other's words. Let me know if you want me to send you the poem I wrote when we were together.

July 25, 2014

Dear Bahareh,

I hope this email finds you well. Attached, please find the interview notes as published today in PDF on our student forum. I apologizing for delaying in making them available but here they are now!

Lastly, these are the questions we still had that remained. We are not seeking answers as you were more than generous with us with you time but I thought they could come in handy to you at a later time:

1. On your website you wrote: "Please remember that it is best to listen with your eyes and look with your heart. That is when you truly start to see the elegance of a spider spinning his web." What do you mean when you say "listen with your eyes and look with your heart"?

2. Is it difficult to be a woman in the UAE? Do you experience challenges exercising your job as a woman in Dubai ?

3. Do you have you any advice for someone who wants to begin writing poems?

4. What are your projects for the future? Where do you foresee yourself to be in ten years from now?

I wish you and yours a fantastic summer and do hope we'll meet in person someday.

Gratefully yours,

A

July 27, 2014

Oh my Dear Dear A,

Hello, what a gift, what a gift of hearts and pure minds. Thank you for this, please please send my love and gratitude to ALL.

And yes, I too hope we will meet one day. I know there is a reason for every path to cross, and so there is indeed a reason for this meeting here now.

Please know that my time is your time, I am so happy to have had this experience with you and your wonderful students. I hope that the gift of writing continues to flow...

I have put together a small booklet of poems as prompts, if you ever want let me know and I will forward it to you.

As for now, the questions that remained, I would love to answer them, for I learn so much from these wonderful thoughtful questions.

1. What do you mean when you say "listen with your eyes and look with your heart"?

Why do I say listen with your eyes and look with your heart.... it is because the heart does not discriminate with color or race or religion or wealth, the heart is simply accepting of love, life and light... and so one can see clearer the gifts of the world. If one were to listen with one's eyes.... one would not hear the noise.... but only simply the sounds of and wonder of life....

To tell you the truth, this is the first time I am thinking about that statement, but it really does make sense now that I write about it.

2. Is it difficult to be a woman in the UAE? Do you experience challenges exercising your job as a woman in Dubai?

I do not experience any challenges as a woman. To be honest, I have found being myself has opened so many doors in my work for me. I guess where there is pure intention and heart, the doors open.

Another thing that can help is that I never identify myself as a woman, I identify myself as a being, and so I am comfortable in all situations.

3. Do you have you any advice for someone who wants to begin writing poems?

Yes, my advice is Just Do it.... (I think Nike copied me)

But seriously, I would simply say just get a piece of paper a pen and open your heart... Do not ask why. Do not stop yourself. Know that the paper will receive what the heart has to tell. Poetry flows and flows only when we allow it to breathe.

4. What are your projects for the future? Where do you foresee yourself to be in ten years from now?

I love this question, it is so well, it is... perhaps so needed for me at this time in my life.

I am not one who plans years ahead of time. However, that does not mean that I do nothing. I am a doer.

I know when things need to be done when they do. Like now I know that my presence is so needed in my immediate family, but also an opportunity has come up possibly to work with a group bringing the arts to hospitals around the world. They have asked me to be the team poetry therapist. To this I say YES.

Where do I see myself ten years from now.... I see myself here now...I hope to be PRESENT where ever I am.

One thing for sure though is that I would like to pass on this gift of poetry as healer to as many people as I can.

Truly yours,

In Light,

Bahareh

Meeting Mother and Baby by Taxi Stand

Abu Dhabi – February 2014

I was planning on going to the Qasr Al Hosn Festival in Abu Dhabi. My husband was traveling to Scotland visiting our eldest daughter, and our younger daughter was in Doha for football, so it was me on my own.

I started walking from our apartment as the festival was close by. Before going there, I wanted to stop at a shop and look at some dishes I had seen earlier. I went into the shop, looked around for a bit and said I would be back. As I stepped back outside, right by the bus and taxi stand, I saw a lady with a stroller. I could not see the baby inside as the top was covering the baby. The mother had tears coming down her cheeks.

I stopped. "May I do anything at all?" I asked.

She wiped off her tears and said, "A taxi just drove off with my purse. I had everything in there. I asked the driver to keep the meter running and wait, and I went to pick up my daughter from the babysitter. When I came back outside, the taxi was gone."

I stood around not really knowing what to do. I asked if she had called the police, and she said yes. I asked if she had called the taxi company, and she said she was trying. She seemed to be having a problem calling, which I discovered to be that she had no credit on her phone. As much as I insisted to send her some from my phone, she refused. We went into the shop with the nice shop keeper, and we used his phone. Then we went back outside.

"Do you want me to stay with you until the police or taxi company calls you back?" I asked.

"Yes," she said politely. "If you don't mind."

The good thing is that the lady (who I found out was named Lamia and was from Morocco) spoke Arabic, so she was able to speak to the police when they called her back. The taxi company also called her back and said she needed to come to the taxi station at the end of Delma Street.

I asked Lamia if she wanted me to go with her. I told her it would be a pleasure. I also told her that my family was out of town so having her company was a delight. I then asked if she wanted me to go to the taxi station with her. She gave the same response as before, and I was more than happy to go with her. All the while, the baby did not make a sound. I peeked through and saw her cuteness with her curls and earrings, but she was deep asleep. I offered to go get my car, but Lamia suggested we go with a taxi.

"They will all know the station, and we will not get lost," she said. Lamia was right.

Lamia and the baby sat in the back seat. I sat in the front and started talking to the nice taxi driver. I was telling him about the festival since we were driving by it. I asked if he had gone, and he said no.

"Can anyone go?"

I said sure, it is only 10 DHS, and you will hear great music, see dancing, the camels, horses, falcons, and more.

"Will I be allowed in with my uniform?"

"Of course you will, but you might feel fresher if you put on another shirt after work," I said. He had a big smile on his face.

He was from Nepal, and I told him how beautiful I thought the people from his country are, how beautiful they are inside and out. I tried to include Lamia in the conversation a couple of times, but I could tell she needed some space.

Shortly after we got to the taxi station, the baby started to wake up. I paid the taxi driver, and I gave him a bit extra saying, "This is so I can be sure you promise you will go to the festival." He laughed.

We went into the taxi station office where the nice lady that Lamia had spoken to on the telephone was waiting at the door to greet us. By now the baby was fully awake. I was happy. When we got in, there was the runaway driver and Lamia's purse and jacket on a table. I could not understand the words, but by her tone, I could tell she was she was asking the taxi driver why he left. He told that she took too long. They were busy with the discussions so I asked if I could pick up the baby. Her name was Kenzie and she was eight months old, a gorgeous baby. I had so much fun holding her and loving her and getting love back. She was really such a good-natured baby.

Her mother Lamia checked the contents of the purse, and the taxi driver got up. He had this thing about him, as though he was not apologetic at all. Anyhow, he left, Lamia signed some papers, we were there for a bit longer, and then went out to find a taxi. The taxi company called for one, but it still took a long time. Finally the taxi came, and I went to Lamia's apartment building with her. I got out, said I would walk around a bit and then catch a cab, and that is exactly what I did. Oh, and Lamia insisted on paying for the first taxi.

I dropped mother and daughter off happily. Lamia told me the hotel she works at, and said I must come and have tea with her.

A week later, I was at the shop with my husband looking at the dishes, and as we stepped out, there was the stroller with Kenzie, fully awake, and smiling, being pushed by a babysitter. I said hello to the little girl and introduced myself to the babysitter.

"Oh, you know Kenzie?" she asked.

"Yes, we met last week," I told her. "Say hello to Lamia for me!"

A day or two later, I went to pick up the china and the shop keeper asked me about the lady that was sad because of her bag. I told him the story and he shook his head.

"Such human beings," he said. "There are not such human beings around."

At first I did not hear him, but he repeated in amazement, "You know these days, no one has time for another person."

"Well, I had nothing better to do, and I was all alone anyhow," I said.

"That is not the point. It's about giving time to another human being."

We both smiled. I helped him put the dishes in my trunk and I drove off from the same place the taxi had driven off with Lamia's purse a week before.

This was such a beautiful experience, it felt so real. When Lamia thanked me, I did not know why she was thanking me, I thanked her for allowing me this space and time to be there with her and her beautiful daughter.

It was truly a gift, delicate like fine china plates.

The Lost Children in the Park

Abu Dhabi – Fall 2014

On a beautiful spring evening, before it got dark, I went out for a walk by the water, through the family park. It must have been a Friday, since it was such a busy night. Families with their little barbeques, kids on bicycles and skateboards, and a lot happening with great energy on a beautiful night.

As I started walking toward the outskirts of the main park, it got quieter. There were not as many kids and families picnicking. I noticed three young children, between ages four and six, happily walking toward something. One of them was older and was leading the way. I stopped walking and stood aside to see if a parent or babysitter or an older sibling would come up behind them. No one came, and the kids kept trotting along. Curious, with a comfortable distance between us, I followed them.

As we were walking, I was amazed at the fun they were having. They seemed so confident. I also kept wondering where their parents were and how they could have left them alone for so long.

They walked for a few more minutes until they got back to the heart of the park, where there were some jungle gyms, climbing bars, tunnels, and a little play area in the sand that looked like a ship. They were on their own little adventure. Yet still, no one was looking for them, nor looking at them. I, however, was looking all around.

I sat at the edge of the sand pit and watched them along with the other kids. Now dusk was turning to dark, and I was getting worried. I thought I would go and say hello to the kids and ask them where their parents were. Quickly, I found out that we did not speak the same language: they did not speak a word of English, and I did not speak a word of Arabic.

I started the search. At first, I asked the man I had been sitting beside, who was watching his daughter, if he spoke English. He said no. Then I went a bit further to a bench with two ladies sitting on it. Both of them spoke English, and one, a nanny for a local family, spoke Arabic. She was from Ethiopia, but had learned Arabic after years of being with the Emirati family. I explained the situation to her, and all three of us approached the kids.

"Where are your parents?" the kind Ethiopian nanny asked them.

The eldest one pointed and said, "That way." I was not sure where "that way" was.

We looked like we were all on an adventure now. The kind nanny picked up the youngest one while I held her hand, and the six of us started walking. I kept eyeing the picnic areas as we passed them to see if anyone might be looking for their children, but saw no one.

To me, it seemed like we had walked for miles, even though it had been little more than a few minutes. At the other end of the park, the little one said, "hanak", meaning "over there" in Arabic.

"Sister, is this your child?" the kind nanny asked, as we approached the woman the kids had pointed out. The mother took the youngest child without a smile or a hint of concern or gratitude. It was as if she had not missed her kids for the entire time they had disappeared.

Grateful that the kids had been safely returned, the kind nanny and I hugged and thanked each other. I was also thankful that I had found a companion for the little adventure we had been on.

It was a beautiful night, and I still smile thinking of the three carefree little ones.

What a Simple Elastic Can Do

Abu Dhabi Sheikh Khalifa Medical Center – September 2015

A friend's daughter, Lori, was staying at the psychiatry ward for care for a few weeks. From time to time, I would go to visit her. I would greet all the other lovely ladies staying there too, and say hi to all the nurses. It felt quite homey and comfortable to be there.

On that particular day, as I was leaving, Lori came to the door with me to say goodbye. Another one of the ladies also came along. Her name was Sophia, and she was in and out of there for a while and did not get many visitors. She could speak a bit, but it was more of a mumble in Arabic, so I did not really understand any of it. However, she managed to communicate by showing. She showed me Lori's hair band and then pointed to herself. The hair band was this kind of plastic coil. To me it seemed like any other hair band. I reached for my hair and took out my regular hair band and asked Sophia if it was okay. She accepted it, and I did not think much of it...

After a couple of days, I went for another visit. As soon as I signed in and put my things in the locker, I was greeted at the door by Sophia. She pointed to her head and then to mine and then to Lori's, who had just walked up.

"Oh, you still want one of those," I said, "I am sorry, I thought the one I gave you was fine." Turning to Lori, I asked if she could give Sophia hers, but Lori said she really needed it, so I reached for the clip I had in my hair. This was not what Sophia wanted, and she would not take it. After a while, Lori took the clip and gave the plastic coil hair band to Sophia, and everyone was happy.

We went into the common room and I did all my visiting and talking and hugging. Then I left to run a few errands, including one to the mall, where I could look for the special hair band. I asked around everywhere, until someone finally suggested the right place to look for them. I bought a few packs, each with five or six in them, and happily took the hair bands back.

As I entered, I thought, why not share with others? I gave one to Mary, the guard at the door. I gave a couple to the young ladies from Nepal who kept the area clean and tidy and were always smiling. Then I went to find Sophia. She had fallen asleep by the TV in the common room, so I left one on the table near her.

I looked for Lori. She was playing cards with her mom in the visitor's room. Asking her to pass them on as she saw fit, I gave her the rest of the goods and said goodbye. On my way out, Mary showed me her hair with the hair band in it.

"I like it," she said with a smile.

There is such joy in simple things. Next time I went, a number of patients showed me their hair bands with smiles all around. The simple truths and beauties of life.

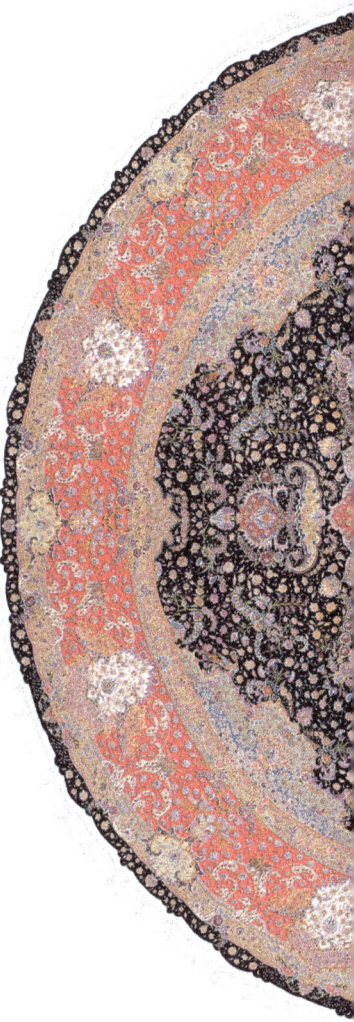

The Beautiful Smile: The Chipped Tooth

Abu Dhabi – August 2013

My eldest daughter and I had gone out to run some errands before stopping at a coffee shop to have lunch. As soon as we sat down, a lovely waitress brought us the menus. She had a very big smile that seemed to come from deep inside. I always sense a genuine smile comes from within, and is not attached to the way a person looks. What made hers even more genuine was her chipped front tooth.

Later, as we were ordering our food, I could not help but mention what a beautiful smile the young lady had. She gave an even bigger smile.

We had our lunch and paid the bill. I told my daughter to go ahead and that I would be out in a minute. I went back to the young waitress so I could ask for her number, explaining that I just wanted to keep in touch with her. She kindly wrote it down for me.

That evening, I called her and we chatted for a while. I mentioned to her that I used to have a chipped tooth, and getting it fixed had made a difference in my smile. The only reason I told her this was because I knew a group of dentists here that could help her out if she felt like it. I thought her smile was incredibly beautiful regardless of the chip.

"Oh," Franka said kindly. "This is now part of my character, I am fine with it."

She went on to explain how it had chipped when she was a young girl when her brother pushed her over during a fight. I realized that the chip in her tooth was important to her, so I didn't press the matter.

"Just let me know if you ever change your mind," I said simply.

And so, a few days passed and she called. She said she had decided to have her tooth fixed. Excited, and happy for her, I asked if I could stop by the next day and take some pictures to show the dentist.

After having the pictures developed, I called a few dentists who were acquaintances of mine. The first one said he was out of town. The next one said he was not sure if he could fix it for free. Finally, I took the pictures to a German lady dentist, who I knew did this sort of thing all the time.

"Sure!" she said, after looking at the pictures. "Bring her here, no problem."

She is an incredible person who is always happy to do complementary treatments for people who cannot afford it. Two days later, I picked up Franka and brought her to the dentist.

"Will it hurt?" she asked. She had never been to a dentist before and I could see why -- she had perfect teeth.

"I'm not sure," I replied, "but I don't think it should hurt."

Franka was not gone for very long before she came proudly out of the dentist's office, with a big smile on her face. The same smile that caught my eye in the coffee shop was still there, just with a sparkly makeover.

She asked to look at herself in the mirror again.

Vahid by the Sea

Abu Dhabi – April 2016

———— I was walking by the sea: the magical sea that carries so many gifts, so many secrets, and so many truths. A man was sitting, upright and bright, on a perfectly laid out cloth. I observed him and went along, continuing my walk. On the way back, I saw the same man, whose name I would later find out is Vahid, and was drawn by the huge tattoo on his back. It looked like a very intricate design.

"Hello. I was drawn by your tattoo," I said, as I walked closer to him.

"What do you see?"

"Nothing in particular," I answered, "but somehow I see light."

"Come sit for a while," he said, motioning me over.

And so I did. As we talked, we discovered that we were both on the same journey in search of light: the journey of inner pilgrimage and the journey of trust in the universe and trust in life. His bag was filled with fresh fruit, and he offered me some.

His body was perfect, with beautiful blue eyes that were most definitely gifted by divine light.

We kept in contact by text message. He had noticed that one of my profile pictures was of a collection of elephant statues. A month or two later, when he came to my book launch, he brought me an elephant as a gift.

Vahid gave me the gift of realizing that moments count, and encounters are real messages showing me that I am on the right path; the path of here and now.

Young Wise Teacher

Abu Dhabi – July 2016

———— I had gone at the regular time to our regular headquarters to meet my mentor for our regular cup of tea. We sat, sipping our moments together through the steamy aroma of our drinks. Moments of joy were shared, as well as other devoid of complete joy.

At one moment, as we were speaking, listening, and considering, sharing a raisin scone, a wise and young teacher appeared before us in the form of a young boy. He seemed to be around five years old, but was in fact, in his wisdom, fifty years old.

We played a game of look and seek. Looking into each other's eyes and seeking the beauty in each other's souls. At first it appeared a simple exchange of glances between mentor, student, and the wise one. Then, the boy went around and looked through two layers of glasses directly into my soul as if seeking my direct attention. I received and reciprocated the gaze that was so intense it made me shy. My mentor was witness to all. Then, after the intense, moment-

long encounter, he ran away. I was not sure to where or to whom or what he was running, and I found myself suddenly jumping up from my chair and following him with my gaze and with my heart.

He had run to a safe place with another adult and a few children. The person that had been standing with him at first observed this last brief moment and thanked me with heartfelt gratitude for keeping an eye. It was really he who was keeping an eye on me. He had come in at that moment in time perhaps to make me realize, in front of my lifelong mentor, that these incredible encounters do not always happen to all. It was as though I was being reminded of this beautiful gift I have been given. I realized that if I share enough of these encounters with others, they will too begin to see the beauty in each and every gaze.

I thank thee for this moment. I thank my teacher and mentor for helping me see the lessons that were being taught by the young wise one through the glass. No imaginary boundaries or borders, just simple connections of heart and soul.

Meeting Saffron

Abu Dhabi – September 2013

There are some encounters whose roots go back many years. This is one of those encounters. I had been afraid of cats for as long as I can remember. The entire family knew we would never be able to have a cat as a pet.

After a terrifying incident that involved a cat emerging from under my car while I was taking the girls to school one morning, I felt I needed to get over this fear of mine and make friends with the cats.

From that day on, I started talking to the alley cats and the cats in the garage, just saying "hello," "how are you," and other such pleasantries.

After a while, I noticed a really skinny cat in our garage who had some kittens close by. I started buying some food and leaving it for the mother. All my communication up to this point had been from far away, hoping that the conversations with cats would ease my fears.

One day I was going to pick up the girls from school and I was a bit early, so I went to the British Vet close by and asked if they had any pets for fostering. They said no, but they had one cat for adoption.

They asked me if I wanted to see it and I very reluctantly said yes. I went to the back room and found the small cat in a cage.

"Do you want to hold it?" asked the vet.

"No," I said very, very firmly.

The cat was placed on the floor, and sat there shyly. Her name at the time was Bean. She was an orange-colored Persian cat, and, I must admit, was very cute. I took a couple of pictures of her, said goodbye, and left.

When I picked up the girls, I told them about what I had done and showed them the pictures.

"Mom, please can we go see her?" they said. "We just want to see her and nothing more!"

Of course, the girls insisted we take the cat home as soon as they saw her, but I said no because this was a big decision that we had to think about. My husband was traveling at the time, so we sent him pictures and told him all about it.

When we got home, the girls kept insisting that we could not leave the cat there for another night. She had already been at the vet for six weeks, which was surprising because she was so cute.

So my lovely daughters promised they would feed the cat, clean the litter box and also wash the dishes and, and, and.... if we could get the cat. Of course, my heart was already taken so we went and picked her up and bought all the necessities.

The cat is now named Saffron, or Saffy. She is a joy to have around for all of us. I cannot imagine what life used to be like without her. I must admit that for a couple of weeks I did not really touch her or get close to her, but now, I cannot get enough of her kind, gentle cuddles.

How lucky I am to be able to have this love in my life. I guess a pinch of Saffron adds flavor and color to everything.

Meeting Khadija Through My Website

Abu Dhabi – September 2014

I was surprised when I got an e-mail on the account connected to my website from a woman who had just moved to Abu Dhabi recently from England. She said she was searching the web for a place where there would be talk of spirituality. Something had led her to my website, and she knew we had to connect.

A couple of days after the e-mail, she came over for tea. She arrived with a glorious bouquet of flowers. We greeted each other as soul sisters do, as if we had known each other since the beginning of time and just now had reconnected.

We sat and drank tea and shared stories about our families. I could tell she was hesitant about the move, but she was going to give it a try. Her biggest concern was for her teenage son that had special needs. She really wanted him to be able to find things to do and to find his place in this desert away from home.

The next time we met was at a coffee shop in the mall. I had the pleasure of meeting her son, Tahir. He is a glorious young man, with the biggest smile. He had on a pair of sunglasses that he slowly took off when he got a bit more comfortable with "auntie" Bahareh. Tahir needs help doing things, but the thing he does best, and which he does all by himself, is exude love and light through his open heart.

It is truly incredible how much a smile can say. It is truly incredible how much one can receive through an open heart. That day we bonded, but then again, I think we had bonded sometime long before that. I could see his point of view on so many things, as my eldest daughter is the same age as him. Tahir is in a body that does not allow him to do all the things his brain and his heart want him to do.

Abu Dhabi is not an easy place to live for someone with special needs. There are not many activities nor are there any publicly accessible places. Small things, like opening doors, become big things in this country.

Kadija and I tried to think of things Tahir could do. Knowing that he was of university age, I thought of classes at an American university that had just opened here. I asked my dear friend, Pamela, if Tahir could sit in on one of her classes, and she agreed. Tahir and his mom ended up sitting through a whole course during the summer and another course in the fall. Kadija openly admitted that she may be enjoying the class more than Tahir was, but I think they both loved the environment and the energy. They often stayed for lunch at the university and made a day of it. Apparently, the other students were wonderful and spent time talking to Tahir, making him feel welcome.

Kadija told me that Tahir was so happy with this situation, as is she. And I... well, I have thanked my friend, Pamela, for allowing this space for growth and flight to happen.

The Ice Cream in the "Not Allowed" Space

Abu Dhabi – September 2015

Before going to meet a friend of mine for lunch, I had gone to the washroom to wash my hands. There was a cleaning lady that I had not seen before so I simply said hello and asked how she was before I went about my way.

After a long lunch and some writing time, I said goodbye to my friend and she went on her way. I was debating whether or not I should have some delicious traditional Syrian ice cream. They gave me a sample, and I got one dipped in pistachios. I convinced myself that the sample is all that I really needed and went on my way, walking around the mall a bit and trying on a pair of sports shoes, which I did not buy.

Before going to the parking, I thought I would use the washroom one more time. She was still there, in the same position with the same sweet eyes and beautiful smile.

I stood by her for a while. She stayed close to me, and we chatted about where we were from and our names and life and such. She had only been in Abu Dhabi for seven months.

"Do you like it here?" I asked her.

"Yes," she replied pleasantly.

I was happy to hear this, but of course a part of me felt bad for the circumstances of her job. However, she was rejoicing and so I joined in with her.

Her name was Nellie and she was from Kenya. She wore the most gorgeous gold eyeshadow above her beautiful eyes. The way she did her eyeliner and her lip liner was like a divine artist.

"You are like a makeup artist," I told her. She smiled. I took out my makeup case and showed her my lone lipstick that also doubled as blush. "I have very little makeup."

"I'll do yours one day," she said.

She said she was not allowed to bring her things to work, not allowed to have a telephone for her entire twelve hour shift, not allowed.... I sat on top of the basin as we continued to talk.

"This is probably not allowed," I said, laughing. She laughed too, so I jumped down. "Can we eat here? Or is it not allowed," I asked.

"If we are eating something together it might be okay," she responded.

"Do you like ice cream?"

"Yes!"

By that time, I had been showing her pictures of my cat and the girls on my phone. I left it with her so she could be entertained and went out and got two special Syrian ice creams with pistachio and two waters.

I hopped back onto the not allowed space. We giggled like little girls and ate our ice cream with joy, slowly, like we had nothing else to do in the world. A couple of people came and left, and we kind of glanced at them and then went back to our beautiful joyous ice cream and story time.

Nellie worked six days a week, 12 hours a day. The only breaks she took were to eat, but she had to go upstairs to a special room.

"Can you walk around the mall during break?" I asked.

"Not allowed."

I laughed so hard that I dropped the cup of ice cream. We laughed even harder as Nellie picked it up. Even though it had fallen upside down, nothing had fallen out.

"After all, it's not allowed to get ice cream on the floor," I said. The ice cream is like elastic and stretches, gooey and creamy, when pulled with a spoon, which is why it did not fall out of the cup. We continued to eat and smile.

I noticed her smile had a little spot on it. I asked about it, and she said she had had it since she was little.

"They say it is from the water where I grew up," she said. "I have always wanted to fix it but it costs too much."

"I had a chip in my tooth, and it was done so well that no one can see it," I told her. "Can I take a picture and show it to my friend who is a dentist?"

"Sure," she replied.

I will always remember the beautiful time we shared. I do not think I have ever enjoyed a scoop of ice cream so much in life, and I know I have never laughed so much about something that is not allowed. I guess no matter where we are in life, we have a choice to make the best of it, unless, of course, it is not allowed....

The Singing Lady Who Had So Much to Say

Abu Dhabi – September 2015

I went to visit a friend's daughter at the Sheikh Khalifa Medical Center's Ward 2. This is where the ladies stayed under supervision, some with mild cases of depression, bipolar disorder, or schizophrenia, and others with not so mild cases. On this particular day, I arrived early and sat in the cantina with my friend for a cup of tea and some goodies she had brought for her daughter. Slowly, we made our way to the ward, but we were still early, since visiting hours started at 10:00 am.

The clock struck ten, and we made our way in, past Mary the security guard, to my friend's daughter, Lori, who was sleeping. As we were going toward her room, my friend pointed out a lady that had come in a few days ago, and was constantly talking to herself or to someone she thought she was talking to. I was told that she did not stop talking all day long, unless she was eating.

Lori woke up, and we all ended up in the common room. In one corner of the room, there was a nurse sitting next to a lady from Bangladesh, who did not seem happy at all. She was all curled up, so I went and sat next to her and touched her back. I held her hand and looked at her painted nails, which were each a different color. She touched each of my fingers, then started to crack my knuckles. It felt funny but cute. When she was done, I wanted to crack hers too, but she waved no. On the other side of the room, sat the talking lady, who was watching TV and talking the whole time. The other conversations continued.

All of a sudden, I saw the talking lady shaking her shoulders. I worried that she was crying, so I jumped up and went to sit next to her. When I got there, I saw that she was laughing, so I started laughing with her. When the laughing was over, we talked for a bit. Her English was good enough to understand, and I found out that her name was Amana and she was 50 years old, despite looking young. When I said I was from Iran, she asked me to sing her a song in Farsi.

I started to sing a song by Googoosh about a long-lost love that appeared again. When I finished singing, she started to sing a song that was half Farsi and half something else, but I understood completely. She finished and I clapped for her. I heard a couple of ladies in the back making comments, so I said, "Oh, you like Amana's singing?"

"You have discovered a new talent," one of them responded.

"Yes, we are here to discover talents," I said. "Amana, would you like to turn around and sing for the others?"

We turned our chairs around so that we were all in a circle facing each other and waited for her to prepare. She started singing a song in Arabic. It sounded like a song of longing. The other Arabic speaking ladies were nodding their heads, and we were all enjoying the voice of the singing lady.

After a little while, we asked others to sing. No one sang, so my friend suggested we all sing happy birthday, and most of us did. Then someone asked me to sing and I sang the same song as before, explaining what it was about first. The talking lady sang a grand finale with lots of clapping and snapping of fingers. One lady wanted to dance but she had hurt her hip.

I had a beautiful visit and later in the day, I spoke on the phone with my friend, who said her daughter was to be released. We talked for a while about the day, and she said, "Bahareh, after you left, that lady did not speak like that again, it was as if she was cured, it was like you had healed her."

I heard her words, and took them in, but I am sure it will take me some time to know exactly what they mean. For now, I will always rejoice with the singing voice of the angel who had so much to say and so much to give.

The Picture Perfect Story

Abu Dhabi – April 2016

I had just started my morning walk when I saw a woman taking pictures of her son, who looked like he was about four or five years old.

"Would you like me to take a picture of the two of you?" I asked, since I never seem to be able to mind my own business.

"Yes," she said, and so I took a few pictures of the two together. The little boy was so cute that I wanted a picture with him too. I did not have my phone or a camera with me, so I asked her if she wouldn't mind sending me the picture of the little boy and me.

We stood around for a few minutes after the mini photoshoot and talked about life. She was considering moving to Abu Dhabi, since her husband already lived here for work, but she sounded apprehensive and unsure.

"We've been here for 8 years and it has been a great place to raise children," I told her.

I gave her my email address and said a big goodbye. It was as if we had known each other for years.

She did send me the pictures: the ones of the two of them, him alone, and me and him together. I was delighted to see his beautiful smile. I was so delighted that I wrote a few lines and emailed them to her:

> *Dear Beatrice,*
>
> *Such a pleasure meeting you both*
>
> > *Mother and son walking by the beach*
> > *One holding the other's hand*
> > *and the other holding the universe in his being*
> > *I come walking along*
> > *I am graced with such presence divine*
> > *I am thankful for the smile, for the talk, for the breeze*
> > *I am thankful to Samuel for letting me pick him up and feel his weight*
> > *His real weight carried in his eyes*
>
> *The mother and the son*
>
> *I am blessed to have met you on this day by the Persian Gulf.*
>
> *Love*
> *InLight*
> *Bahareh*
> *Thank you for gracing my day*

I did not hear back from her and did not think anything of it. Then, on June 30th, over two months after our chance encounter, I received this email:

> *Good Morning from Nigeria!!!*
>
> *It's been a while! Hope the family and yourself are great? You won't believe it but I never knew it was from iCloud I sent the first mail. Just reading your now and I feel really really really good! (Emphasis mine).*
>
> *Yea, the young Sammy is fine. We are soaking in my plenty of vitamin D and other fruits and food vitamins naturally from Nigeria. We came the 3rd day of June and will finally be moving to join my spouse in Abu Dhabi come October.*
>
> *Our chanced meeting though brief made impact in our lives. You don't have to know someone for decade for impact to be felt, thanks Amidi for the wonderful poem. It's soooo touching!!! Guess you must be in America by now or you moved finally to Europe cos you told me you were moving the Month of June.*
>
> *My warm regards to your family. And I wish you Heavens best. Hugs and kisses,*
>
> *Beatrice!!!*

I wrote back a day or two later:

> *Dearest Beatrice,*
>
> *Hello and thank you so much for this email.*
>
> *I know sometimes emails gets lost in the Cloud....hehe.... but the love felt is never lost.*
>
> *I am glad you are enjoying the sun, the food and I am sure the love, kisses to both of you.*
>
> *You have a great memory... yes, we should have moved by now, but we are still here, not sure when the move will happen.... but in fall I think... maybe another chance encounter :)*
>
> *Meeting you also was such a touching experience for me.... thank you, may you always be so blessed and shed your light around.*
>
> *Actually I am putting together a book of encounters ... chance encounters that have touched my life. I would love to use this story.... of our meeting, especially if you tell me more about the "impact" as you say.*
>
> *Thank you truly and always*
>
> *With love*
>
> *In Light*
>
> *Bahareh*

On July 4th, she wrote back:

> *Dearest Bahareh,*
>
> *Thank you so much for getting back. Am also thanking God for sustaining you and your loved ones with the breath of life till another chance encounter in the near future. Life is a matter of time and chance but we always pray to be in the right place when the chance will happen.*
>
> *Bahareh, there was this positive vibes or aura around you that made every thought SURE. All I felt was 'I can achieve anything if I just set my mind on it'. This is so because as soon as you said you were relocating I had this flash of doing another course ending up in another profession other than the Law degree I am presently with. I had struggled with this because I felt I needed to make another baby and I will be too old but your single utterance of "if God permits" or "InshAllah" put a seal on it. I have started scouting for schools in the USA now for a Nursing degree hahhahaha. This much is the impact, so help me God to achieve same.*
>
> *Conclusively, the aforementioned was the reason I said you don't have to know someone for decades before they make impact in your life especially positive ones. Thanks Darling, regards to you and your family. Love and kisses,*
>
> *Beatrice*

That same day I replied:

> *Dearest Beatrice,*
>
> *Thank you for this gift, for the gift of light and the gift of flight.*
>
> *Thank you for sharing your thoughts with me, and also for being so open to receive love and Light.*
>
> *I am touched by what you tell me, and I must say it is your energy and the way you were with your son that drew me to you.*
>
> *I suppose all three of us were we needed to be at the right time.*
>
> *Many many blessings. Let us see one another if possible when you return. Good luck on your future adventures where-ever they may take you.*
>
> *With love,*
>
> *In Light,*
>
> *Bahareh*

Such beautiful situations can unfold if we are open, if we are aware, and if stand aside and let pictures and images come to life.

Hebe From Sudan

Abu Dhabi – February 2014

Even though I was going for the second night in a row, I took a taxi to the Qasr al Hosn Festival to enjoy the good energy, the music, the dancing, and the food that brought people together. I walked around for a while, talking to a few members of the production crew and enjoying the festive atmosphere.

I wanted to stop walking for a while and sit to enjoy the sights and sounds. Seeing a bench, I walked towards it, deciding to sit down even though there was already another lady on it. It was not a big bench so there was only a little bit of empty space between us.

"Are you waiting for someone?" I asked her, trying to start a conversation.

"No, I am here alone," she said, a tinge of sadness in her voice.

"I am here alone, too."

As we got to talking, I found out why she was so sad to be alone. She wished her children could be there to enjoy this time with her. Her kids were 10 and 12. They used to live in Abu Dhabi with her husband before she divorced him because of his drinking problem. He would not let the children stay with her, and she needed a job so she ended up living alone. Her name was Hebe, which she said meant "giving and giving and giving". I found out that it could also be translated into "blessing".

I suggested we go get a cup of coffee, but she said she was fine on the bench.

"Besides," she said. "Is it free?"

"Let's go get a cup of tea," I said a while later. "We will go see what happens."

She agreed to this, so we started walking. It was so pleasant, really, as if we had known each other for years, but without any of the baggage that weighs down lifelong friends.

Eventually, we got to a little tea shop I had seen the night before. It was an old-style tea shop, where we could sit indoors or out by the street. Hebe went inside and sat so I followed her in, even though I kind of wanted to sit outside and people watch.

I asked the other ladies in the shop what they were eating, and they said the shop was out of food.

"We just need two small servings," I said with a smile.

I paid for the food and the tea, and found it all waiting on our table by the time I went back to sit down. We did not know what we were eating, but it was delicious. The ladies in front of us said it was chicken, potatoes, beans, and such, all mashed up. They make something similar in Iran with lamb or beef, called goost kobideh. Hebe asked me how much I paid. I told her, it was really not expensive, 16 dhs for everything. I bought a frozen yogurt at the mall for myself for more than that.

We kept talking as we ate, and she told me she had been to Kish, an Island just off the coast of Iran.

"The women were beautiful there," she said.

"So are Emirati women," said the lady across from us, who had somehow become part of the conversation.

"Yes, so are all women," I added. "We have all been created by the same God."

When we were finished, we went out to a van I had spotted earlier that sold sweets. I stood in line and paid and waited for our dessert. It was divine. We sat on some cushions on the ground as we ate. It was not too comfortable though, so we soon got back up and started walking again.

We reached a man-made pond with a boat on it. It was almost closing time, but there was still a line of people waiting to get on. Hebe wondered if we could get on.

"Sure," I said, "I think it's free, too."

There was an old man with a white beard on the floor of the little boat. He was opening some oysters and explaining something in Arabic. I got off the boat because I was feeling sea sick, even in the bathtub-sized pond, but I saw Hebe's glowing face from across the way, and it made me smile.

"Okay, let's go," she said, getting off the boat after a while with everyone else.

It was 11pm at this point, so we walked out of the festival. Hebe said she would cross the street to catch the bus.

"What are you going to do?" she asked.

"Walk a bit, maybe catch a cab."

We hugged and said goodbye. It was truly sweet.

"You know, when I came here and when I was sitting there, I was thinking of crying," she said, "but now I had such a great time."

I told her that it was the same for me. I was so lonely at first, but when I met her everything changed, and I had a great time, too.

Even if we never speak again, I will always remember the expression of a mother missing her young kids, who could have been at that festival with her. Hebe said that maybe when her kids are 18, she can get them a visa and bring them to Abu Dhabi. I will always remember her big smile, despite it all, with the space between her front teeth that made way for her personality to shine through.

Six Year Old in the Construction Zone

Abu Dhabi – September 2014

On my way to buy something at the small convenience store near our apartment building, I noticed a little girl standing on the sidewalk with her backpack on. I thought she must be waiting for her parent.

On my way back from the store, I noticed the girl was still standing there. I decided to stand by just to make sure she wasn't going to be all alone. I was worried for her, because there were two different construction sites near our building, with trucks and workers and lots of commotion.

Quite a few more minutes passed, and yet the girl was still alone. I walked up to her.

"Hello," I said. "Are you waiting for your mother?"

"I'm waiting for a friend," she answered.

Hmmmmm, I thought. Interesting.

Skeptical, I waited with her. We stood there for about 15 minutes before I realized the friend was not going to show up. With each school bus that came by, the girl would insist that her friend was in it. We would wait with complete certainty, but there would be no friend hopping off the bus once it stopped.

By this point I had figured out that the girl, named Didiyah, was originally from Afghanistan and understood some Farsi. However, it was still easier to communicate in simple English. I asked about her English textbook, and she took it out to show me. We read together (she pointed, I read) for a while. The longer we stood there, the more uneasy I became that this girl was standing alone outside. Her mother must be worried sick by now.

Didiyah told me that she lived in the same building as me, so we got in the elevator together. I was amazed that the girl was so comfortable with someone she did not know.

"Please don't talk to strangers," I told her. "You don't even know if I'm okay to talk to!"

"Can I come see your cat?" she asked, just as I finished telling her not to talk to strangers.

"No!" I said, in shock. "How could you possibly come to a person's home that you do not even know? No, no, no."

I hoped I had scared her so that she would learn not to be so forward with strangers, but my words seemed to make no difference. We went to her door, and she rang the doorbell. I thought her mother would come running to the door, half scared to death, but it was opened by her younger brother, who could not have been older than three. Another brother, even younger than him came to the door, too.

I could hear the mother faintly inside the apartment so I simply said hello.

"I saw your daughter downstairs and I was so scared for her," I said in Farsi.

Her mother responded saying that she was busy and thought that this was such a safe neighborhood that Didiyah could come home from the bus alone.

"I'm not sure how safe it is," I returned. "There is so much construction going on and so many construction workers around, and your daughter was waiting for her friend for a very long time. Since I have two daughters myself, I got worried."

Upon hearing this, her mother was so grateful. "It is as if an angel has come to the door!" she said. I was not quite sure who the angel was exactly, but I was thankful for whatever force it was that had taken me to the convenience store and made me wait with Didiyah. Didiyah and her mom came up to my apartment a few days later to see the cat and chat for a bit. From time to time, I see different family members in the elevator or around the building, and I have also seen the mother waiting for the school bus a few times. Each time I see her, I thank the angel that was with me that day that pushed me to take Didiyah home.

Claire by the Sea

Abu Dhabi – September 2015

I woke up to a beautiful morning that immediately called me to the sea. I got ready and headed out to take a walk and swim in the warm Persian Gulf. We are so fortunate that the sea is a ten minute walk from our apartment. All I have to do is walk out of the front door of our building, make a left into the park, cross the street through an underpass, and there is the water.

I walked a bit further down the beach than I usually do. Someone was lying down by one of the lifeguard chairs so I thought I should go a bit further so as not to annoy them but changed my mind and put my stuff down anyway. As I took off the shirt I had over my bathing suit to go into the water, the person who was lying down, a lady, got up.

"Hello," I said.

"Hello," she replied warmly.

We chatted for a bit, but I could tell there was more talking to do so I sat down near her and played with the sand.

"What do you do?" she asked me.

"I am a teacher and a poet and a therapist. What do you do?"

"I used to work in a shop, but they are not paying my salary, so I stopped. I'm looking for another job now," she said. "I applied for a job as a waitress and I'm waiting to hear back."

I found out that her name was Claire and she was a mother of three and supports them herself. I suggested she take her CV and drop it off at a 100 different places over the next few days.

"If the CV needs to be worked on," I continued, "make it perfect, and then take it."

She smiled. "It is as if I needed a push," she said, "I am happy I met you today."

Eventually I got up to go swimming, asking her if she wanted to join me.

"I don't know how to swim," she answered. "I stay close to the shallow part and play in the water."

"Okay," I said, going into the water.

A little while later, I saw Claire in the water. It looked like she had become more comfortable in the water and in practicing floating with her face in the water. I swam towards her.

"Wow, you do know how to swim," I exclaimed. And as she came up with a smile she said:

"No," she said, "I just put my head in."

She told me that she had been in a boat when she was young and had fallen in, which scarred her. Later in her life, she and her young kids had to run away from her husband on a boat, which also got in an accident. It was due to these traumatic experiences with boats and the ocean that she had not made much progress in learning to swim until now.

"I understand completely," I told her, "but it is great to see you float. There are only two things you need to do to swim: one is to float and the other is to make bubbles."

I started to make bubbles with my face in the water, then turn my head up, then turn it down and make more bubbles, and so on. Claire started making bubbles too, and I made some more, and we kept going for a while like that.

"Now, you float like you did before and keep making bubbles and move your arms and legs and you'll be swimming."

About 15 to 20 minutes later, Claire and I had ventured out a few meters. She was so delighted to see how far she could go with just a few bubbles and some hand strokes.

"Now I can swim!" she said excitedly. "Today is a lucky day. I feel it. Now I will go fix my CV and take it to different places."

I could hear the spark in her voice and see the joy on her face. Her spark stayed with me all day long. Claire by the sea, thank you for your warm hello and for trusting me to hold you while you floated and made bubbles out of the realities of life.

David in the Air

Paris Airport – October 2015

The flight from Frankfurt to Paris was completely packed. I was on my way to Scotland to visit my daughter, and there were a couple of layovers along the way. I had an aisle seat, and there was a gentleman, who I could tell was American, sitting beside me by the window.

"Hello," I said, as I sat down. "Aren't you cold?"

The man had shorts on while I was wearing a cashmere sweater and a coat and was still freezing.

"I prefer to travel this way," he replied casually.

"Yes, my brother travels in shorts and flip flops and always says we do not know what we are missing."

Not much else was said. I closed my eyes and dozed off a bit until take off. Since it was such a short flight, they were only offering things to drink. I asked for tea and water.

"Were you in Frankfurt for the book fair?" I asked the gentleman next to me after a few sips of tea. I was not sure if I asked him that question just to make conversation, or if I was hoping he would turn out to be a publisher or editor who could help with my book. He told me he was a businessman who traveled a lot.

We talked for a while about traveling, and how fortunate we are to be able to travel, but also how nice it is to sleep in one's own bed. He had been on the road for three weeks already.

"Look at that cloud," he said. "It is so different!"

At first I did not see anything particularly interesting, but then I saw the cloud, which looked like a mountain or a volcano. He took several pictures of it.

Wow, I thought. A gentleman who notices clouds, points them out to others, and takes pictures of them. Incredible.

The gentleman, whose name I still did not know, told me how tired he was. He had stayed up all night to watch a football game and a baseball game.

"Oh, you should try to take a nap," I suggested.

"No, I can't sleep now."

I had noticed a tattoo on his ankle when I sat down, and now I saw another one peeking out of his short sleeve shirt. When I mentioned his tattoo, he pulled up his sleeve so that I could see it. There was some design around the arm, which looked like what Jesus wore on his head at the crucifixion.

He turned his body around to show me more tattoos. There was one for his wife, and one for each of his children: the wings of an angel and boxing gloves for his son Cehamp. Then there was another for his mom: two M's with a daisy between them. He told me his mom had been cremated and that there were some ashes in the ink.

"You can feel them," he said. I touched his arm and voiced my amazement. It was quite a personal thing to share, both him telling me about the tattoos and me touching his arm. Touching happens on many different, and sometimes sacred, levels.

"Have you heard the poem about the angel who lost her wings," I asked, thinking about the angel wings he had drawn on his arm.

"No."

"Would you like to hear it?"

"Sure," he said.

So, I began, "Once upon a time, there was an angel, an angel who lost her wings…"

"That was very nice," he said, as I finished the poem, "whose is it by?"

"It's actually one of mine," I replied.

"Wow, I could never write like that," he told me. "I wish I could write something similar."

That is when I turned to a blank page in my notebook. "You can write," I said encouragingly. "You know what writing is? Writing is just seeing this, any blank piece of paper in the world, and knowing it is an invitation to your heart and soul."

I saw his eyes get big and his soul open.

"All you need to do is to open your heart, and let your heart pour out onto the paper," I continued, putting my hands over my heart and making a pouring motion onto the paper.

"Yeah, I really do not know how to write," he said, smiling.

"Yes, but you know what, just look at the blank page, the invitation, and write about two things: your feelings and images that come to you in this very moment."

I saw a sparkle in his eyes, so I tore a piece of paper out of my notebook. I asked him if there was a word or phrase that touched or resonated with him in the poem.

"Yes," he said, "fly."

At the top of his paper I wrote the word "fly" and at the top of mine, I wrote "I sat and sat and sat". I gave him his paper and a pen.

"I am not good at things like this," he started to say, but I cut him off.

"Yes, I know, but just remember the moment."

It seemed like there was a shift in him, and I felt him starting to write. I wrote, and he wrote, and when I stopped and looked up, he was still writing. After a while he stopped too. He looked like he was proud of what he had written.

Before asking him to read it, I explained to him that whatever he wrote would stay between us in our own sacred circle, and would never be judged, but only received with love and respect.

"Okay," he said, and started to read. With each sentence, the tone of surprise and amazement grew in his voice. "That was pretty good!" he said, as he finished reading.

"How did that feel?" I asked him.

"It felt nice to let that come out of me."

I reflected a line from his writing that resonated with me and asked if I could read it back to him before reading my own poem.

My travel companion listened and when I asked him to reflect back a line that resonated with him, he said, "'present doing what I do' and 'in this very moment I find myself once again present.'"

"Wow, this is incredible what we just did," he continued. "Is this what you do? You teach?"

"Yes," I replied, "I am a poetry therapist. I bring this gift to others."

"You enable, you facilitate", he said. I then explained to him the concept of poetry therapy.

"Now I feel like I can just write and write," he said.

I reached into my bag and took some more poetry for us to read. Everything happened so beautifully and without any strain. David was ready for this gift.

"I am going to take this to my family, to my wife, to so many people," said David. "You know what is important about what you do? It is that what you do, does not stop with me, it touches more lives than you can imagine."

David was glowing and his light reflected into my soul. "I am so lucky I sat here today and all the others that did not get this seat on this flight were not lucky," he said. We gave each other a high five and smiled.

Soon, it was time for the descent. We happily said goodbye on the plane and that we would keep in touch. However, we discovered that our gates were close to each other, and so we rode on the shuttle bus together. David kept reminding me of how amazing it was.

"I come from a family of business," I said, "and sometimes these things can be overlooked."

"There are a lot of business men in the world," he replied, "but not many people that do this kind of thing."

I walked David to his gate where he was flying to New York, then sat around in the Paris airport waiting for my own flight, and reminiscing on what had happened a mere hour ago. David had surprised me when he said that the moment on the plane was life changing for him. I was honored.

Well, wingless, we flew, David and I, high above the clouds, arriving to the present moment with the gifts we brought each other; the gifts of presence and reflection.

Sergio, the Man Who Maintains Everything at Valporaiso

California Menlo Park – May 2014

It had been a year since I had joined the Institute for Poetic Medicine. We were a beautifully diverse group of students, both in body and mind, who met at a spot called Valporaiso twice a year for our classes, talks, discussions, soul connections, and learning.

One beautiful evening, at the end of a day of meetings, we had a poetry recital; something simple, plain, deep, and beautiful for ourselves, family, friends, and anyone in the community that wanted to join. A few of my own family members were coming, including my mother and brother, my young niece, and my youngest daughter. It was so kind of them to come and stay through the recital, even though they do not have a real interest in poetry.

After the recital, there was a table set up by a kind friend of the institute's with cheese and wine and grapes and so on. By then, my family members had left. I had spotted Sergio, the wonderful gentleman who helped take care of everything, at the front desk, so I made a nice cheese plate and a drink and took it into the building. I went in and said hello to Sergio and offered him the food. I think he asked me how the program went so I told him it went well. Then I offered to tell him a little bit about the institute and what poetry therapy was. He was very open.

He came around from the desk, and we sat on the couch in the lobby. I asked him if he could kindly bring two blank pieces of paper and two pens. So he did. When we were seated again, I took one of the pieces of paper, and I held it up and said, "This is Poetry Therapy."

He looked confused, so I continued "Any blank piece of paper anywhere in the world, you see, is an invitation to your heart and soul."

A smile from Sergio, told me he wanted to hear more. "All you need to do," I said, "is to open your heart and pour it on the paper. Write about two thing: images and feelings in this very moment now. The only thing I ask you not to do is please do not block anything that arrives. Let it arrive."

I decided to recite a poem for Sergio:

The Angel Who Lost His Wings

Once upon a time there was an Angel

An Angel who lost his wings

He was walking through life wondering what fault had made his wings disappear

He saw the birds flying in the sky and the bees buzzing around

He saw a rock by the window and he sat

and sat

and sat

after years of sitting he decided to walk again and look for his wings

That is when he started to fly

wingless with heart

At the end of the poem, I could see a smile in Sergio's heart, and I knew it was the perfect time for the blank piece of paper. I invited him to write, and he said he really did not know how.

"No worries," I said. "Write in any language, and anything that arrives, do not stop yourself."

We sat together in that beautiful atmosphere of trust and both wrote. Afterwards, we shared our words with each other. It was truly nothing but a gift of the moment. Sergio was absolutely surprised with himself and with what he had written.

I was going to head back to the wine and cheese party, so I asked him if I could have a copy of his poem. He asked me if he could have a copy of mine, so Sergio went back to the desk and made the copies and we exchanged poetry, just as we had exchanged light and trust and flight.

By the time I got back, everyone was smiling at me. A few people said, "Bahareh, did you do one of your capsule poetry therapy sessions?"

"Yes," I replied, adding how magical it had been and who it was with, since everyone knew Sergio. I could tell they were interested in what we had shared. Running back, I asked Sergio if I could share his poem with the others. He said yes with a smile and blush, which to me indicated joy. Everyone was in awe of the poem the words and the beauty...

A year later, I was getting my certification from the Institute for Poetic Medicine. I had only invited a few family members and a friend, who could not come, to the ceremony. I had also invited another friend, Sergio, and told him it would mean the world to me if he came. Seeing him there, I could tell how proud he was of my accomplishment. I was so proud to have him there, remembering the pure moment we had shared that night a year ago. A year later, a friend of mine had gone there for another program, and Sergio had asked her to send me this note:

When I think of an angel I think of you, with smile and open wings ready to embrace the world. May your journey be full of blessings to continue be an inspiration to others.

-Sergio, January 2016.

Lizzy in the Taxi

Dubai to Abu Dhabi – August 2015

I had just come back from visiting my sister in Iran where I had gone to surprise her for her birthday. I had a lovely time. As I was getting into a ladies' taxi at the airport in Dubai, my phone rang. It was my sister, thanking me for coming to visit and making her birthday so special. The driver got on the freeway as we were chatting and started to speed.

"I am not in any kind of hurry. Please drive slowly," I told the driver, excusing myself from my conversation with my sister.

She said okay, but the same thing happened a couple minutes later. I said goodbye to my sister and started talking to Lizzy, the taxi driver. Apologizing for asking her to drive slowly, I told her about my fear of highway driving.

"It is not your issue," I said. "It is simply me."

"No problem," replied Lizzy. "You must be sent from God to remind me to drive slow. I always drive too fast."

We continued to talk about life and family and work. She told me she had been in Dubai for a few years, and that her contract with the taxi company was almost finished. After that, she was going to go back to Cameroon to get married, then come back. She had a 14-year-old daughter there from a previous marriage who was staying with her mother in Cameron. The man she was going to marry was a pastor in a community close by. She had met him 12 years ago in passing, and had only seen him a couple of times since. About three months prior, he found her on Facebook, and they started talking. Shortly after, he proposed to her.

She glowed when she spoke of him, his kindness, and his heart. She did not seem too sure about leaving him and coming back to the UAE to work. I just listened for a while.

"Sweetie," I said a bit later. "Why don't you just stay with your sweetheart in his safe and beautiful arms? Everything will be okay." I mentioned how her daughter needed her now, and how all the money in the world would not replace one minute with her mama.

Lizzy gave out a big sigh, or scream, or laugh of joyous wonder. I could not really tell what the sound she made was, but she said, "Are you an angel? Just tell me the truth!"

Her face became filled with tears, and I asked her to pull over so we could talk. Even though we were on the shoulder of a busy highway, we felt like we were in our own world. I moved to the front seat, and we hugged and prayed together. She sent a message to her love, saying she has for the first time met a real-life Angel.

We hugged a bit more, and then kept praying. She started singing a prayer to her PaPa. She said when she feels close to God, she prays in that voice. We recited the Our Father Prayer, which she could not believe I knew. She asked me what I wanted to pray for, and I told her the health of a particular family member. She prayed with all her might. We both knew our prayers were heard that night. Before heading back, we embraced each other and took a selfie, which I will always cherish. We were both weepy eyed but bright hearted.

After getting back on the road to Abu Dhabi, we kept talking and telling each other stories from our lives. She delivered me safely home to my family. I hope soon PaPa will deliver her safely home to hers.

Mahara, Who Lit a Candle in My Heart

Abu Dhabi – September 2015

I had gone to visit my friend's daughter at the hospital. She was in the psych ward because she was not feeling well. When I entered with my friend, there was a lady in the front greeting us. She had such a beautiful gentle mannerism about her. I thought she must be a therapist, or of a similar profession.

We all flowed into the main area together and sat around and talked. I realized that the lady at the front, whose name was Mahara, was in fact a patient and not a therapist, when she told me how long she had been here and why. Slowly, I started noticing her mannerisms more. She was very slow, quite simply like someone who had been heavily drugged.

After a while, a lady walked in with a plastic bag and dug around inside it. She took out a handful of colored pencils and threw them on the table, without any semblance of attention or kindness. Next she pulled out a few papers and told the ladies to come and color. I felt sick to my stomach by her seeming disregard. Coloring seemed like such an inappropriate and demeaning activity for these grown women, in that moment.

I am not sure why, but I got up and walked toward the table. I was the first to do so. As I was sitting down, Mahara got up and came to the table, too. The picture she chose to color made me smile. It was of a young girl with angel wings, flying above a big cloud with rays of light coming out of it.

I started sharpening the broken colored pencils, but the sharpener kept eating them up and breaking the tips. But we made do. Mahara, a couple of others and I colored, while Mahara and I talked. Her English was perfect and she had gone to university in the UK. She had studied something in relation to education and teaching. She said she was here because of her moods and because she did not like taking medication.

Openly and honestly, I started talking to her about my bipolar diagnosis and my experience with Lithium and other medications. I told her how they affected my life both positively and negatively. She listened eagerly and asked me questions, which I was happy to answer. The only people she really worried about, she said, are her two children. This was something I had experience with, so I told her the only reason I knew I had to take my medicine was for my girls. If I wanted to remain a mother, I had to be militant about the medications and their levels and such. She listened, colored, and nodded.

Soon, coloring time was over and the lady with the plastic bag came and took the pencils and what we had colored. I asked her if we would keep what we colored. She did not seem to care either way; she just wanted to gather up and move on, perhaps to the next ward. Mahara had not yet finished the skirt of the angel, so we asked her to wait a bit before gathering the art supplies.

Almost simultaneously, Mahara and I started writing something on our drawings. I wrote to her with all my heart, saying, "You are the only one that can help yourself and your children, you are strong and wonderful and divine." She wrote wishing me good luck with everything and added, "You have lit a candle in me today."

For this candle I bow my head. I am grateful for the lady with the plastic bag and the broken colored pencils and the ward. I am grateful for the hour that brought the two angels together to help each other fly.

The Cat in the Bag

Abu Dhabi – September 2015

My husband and I had gone out to a casual Indian restaurant for dinner. We enjoyed our food thoroughly. Afterwards, I suggested we take a short walk around. There was a new hotel across the street so I suggested we go and take a look inside.

It was a nice night out. The weather felt like it was transitioning from the usual miserable heat to a beautiful cool temperature. We were enjoying the outdoors and approaching the new hotel when we noticed some young boys playing with a tiny kitten. I stood by for a couple of minutes just to make sure that the cat was not being roughly handled.

The boys took a few pictures with the cat and saw me standing by and went on their way. My husband and I stood around for a while

"Okay, let's go," he said.

"Let us wait a bit and see if the mother will show up," I replied. We waited around, but there was no mother in sight.

I went into a furniture store that was close by and asked if they had seen the kitten's mother, but they said no. Back outside, I found the young boys waiting at the bus stop, and I asked them if they had seen the mother of the cat, but they also said no. I asked them if they wanted to take the kitten home, and they said they couldn't.

When I came back, I found the kitten playing on my husband's lap, feeling quite at home. I ventured off to buy some food for the little one. There was no cat food so I bought some tuna and water.

While at the small grocery store, I asked the owner, who happened to be Iranian, if he wanted a cat. He also said no.

"I can give you a plastic bag if you want to take it home," he told me.

"No thank you," I said, and went off with the tuna and water.

The kitty was so happy with the water and tuna. We took some pictures and sent them to our daughters, telling them the story of the kitten. We called the veterinarian, but there was no response, which made sense at this hour of the night and on a long weekend. Then my husband had the great idea of taking the kitten close to a store where there are a bunch of stray cats and a cat lover, known as the cat lady, who always feeds them there.

Now it was time for me to go and get the plastic bag from the Iranian grocer. He laughed as he gave me a couple of bags.

At first, my husband, tried to carry the kitten in his sweater, but it kept wanting to jump out. Then we put him (we think it was male) into the bag, and that is when all the meowing started. It sounded like a whole family of cats. We rushed toward the car and placed the plastic bag in a bigger shopping bag and kept the bag in the back.

The meowing was so loud that I turned up the music because I did not want to hear the cat's distress. Finally, I suggested I walk home or take a taxi home.

I got out of the car and walked halfway home. My husband called and said that Batman was safely by the grocery store. (We had given him the nickname because of his large ears.) The security guard by the building had said that the Cat Lady had already gone to feed the cats. He said he would watch over the kitten until the Cat Lady came back. My husband bought some food for the kitten and left it there as well.

The next day I called Mary, the Cat Lady, and talked to her. She said the kitten was too small to be on the street, that she had taken him in, and that we need to find him a home. With the help of my daughter, we made some flyers and posted them at school and the store. After a week or so, Mary called me and said the cat, now officially named Phillip, had found a home. Isn't it incredible how beautiful beings come into our lives and touch us in such divine ways?

The Daughter I Did Not Know

Abu Dhabi – April 2016

It was before dinner time, and I felt like I needed to get out of the house for a while and go for a walk. I went to the beach and started to walk by the water, feeling the sand and the waves underneath my feet. A young lady was approaching me with a big smile, asking me if I could take a picture of her. I happily took her phone and took a few pictures of her; some with the water, some with the skyline. I handed her the phone back and she kind of held on to my hand as she said thank you.

I continued on my walk and saw her again on my way back. I could tell she wanted to talk so I asked her if she lived in Abu Dhabi or was a visitor in town. She told me she had moved to Abu Dhabi six months ago, and was now working in a hotel. We started walking by the beach again.

She told me she was from Myanmar and that she was the youngest of seven children. The rest of her siblings were married.

"Your parents must be missing you," I told her.

"No," she said, "my father died when I was 12, and my mother died 23 days after that. I grew up living with one sibling then another, but I eventually knew I had to make my own life, my own way."

She had worked and studied and done all she could to get herself to a place where she would have more opportunities. She had a smile that turned into laughter, and later I thought it was the kind of smile, or laughter, that at times can make me feel sad, like someone trying to hide a lot behind it.

We sat together for a while longer, and talked some more until I remembered it was dinner time for my family and my husband and daughter would be waiting. I said goodbye, and we exchanged phone numbers, kissed, and hugged. As we were parting ways she said "Goodbye Ma'am" I know I had introduced myself by my first name, but that is what she was comfortable with, since it is customary in the UAE.

"Dear Haniya," I said, "You can call me anything but ma'am. You can call me Bahareh or auntie or anything else, but not ma'am."

There was a moment of silence. "Can I call you mom?" she asked.

"Of course you can, that is an honor."

There, I found how much a simple word can mean to someone. A single smile, a single hug, a single moment in time. From that day we kept in touch by Whatsapp, and we met once again in person. When we met, Haniya, my newly found daughter brought me a box of cookies. I showed her around town to a few places she had not yet seen, and we had some afternoon tea together, rejoicing in the moment. It made me realize that walking by the beach, on the street, in a forest, or anywhere, if you cross someone's path, it is always for a reason.

Twins, Born Years Apart

Konya-2017

The great poet Rumi was laid to rest in Konya, Turkey. Every year on December 17th, the anniversary of his death, individuals from all walks of life flock to the site where the peerless laureate is buried. They migrate there not to mourn, but to celebrate, in reflection of his own conviction that, "when I die, that is my true marriage to the beloved".

I had not intended to go on this trip, but sometimes things line up in a way that makes fate feel indisputable. As I had purchased my ticket late, the only seat available was in the final row of the plane, right next to the bathrooms and without the option to recline. Determined to save my back the pain of a long flight sat straight, I asked the steward if I could move to another seat. He told me there were none available and I began to settle in as comfortable as I could. As the plane began to taxi, the same steward came back and said there was one seat available in the front next to an older gentleman. I thanked him, quickly gathered my things, and moved swiftly to the open aisle seat.

As I arranged my belongings, I glanced over to the gentleman sitting next to me and greeted him with "Salam". He introduced himself as Mr. Gilani. We began chatting and soon found ourselves sharing stories spanning lifetimes, as the plane quietly traversed countries. As we were landing, he told me that this was the first flight he had ever been on while conscious. His previous experience with flying was during the Iran-Iraq War, when he was rushed onto a medical airplane after an encounter with Mustard gas which left him with a large scar and facial deformity still immediately apparent on his face so many years later.

As people stood up to collect their bags from overhead compartments, Mr. Gilani mentioned that he had been invited to visit Konya by the Turkish government, after representatives visited the historic site of Tughrul Tower which he helped to maintain. A 12th century monument found in the city of Rey, Iran, Tughrul Tower holds deep significance for the Turkish people.

After collecting our luggage, I noticed that Mr. Gilani was looking around with an air of mild confusion. I asked him who would be picking him up, to which he replied with an unbothered shrug. I decided to stay around for a while to make sure he met his ride. I was relieved when an official-looking driver arrived. As I went to say goodbye, he insisted they give me a ride to my hotel. I ignored the mental image of my eldest daughter scolding me for being naïve about the intentions of strangers, and accepted his invitation.

Before arriving at the hotel, we made a quick stop at the office of tourism and delegation, who had invited the Mr. Gilani to their country. He immediately embraced the official who came out to greet him with the biggest hug. They spoke the same language of love and respect, if not that of their mother tongues.

I quickly become Mr. Gilani's unofficial translator for the duration of the evening, accompanying him to a traditional meal followed by a formal Whirling Darwish Dance. It was a lovely evening made possible by only a chance encounter.

As we parted ways, we arranged a time to meet in the morning. It was such that we spent much of the remaining four days of my trip in each other's company, companions for lunch, dinner, or visiting historic sites. It became evident that this was probably some sort of destiny. I was in Konya that year not only to celebrate Rumi, but also to meet this gentleman. We later learned that we shared a birthday; March 21st, the first day of spring and the Persian New Year.

He became steadfast in the stance that we were most definitely twins, somehow separated by years and lands and seas until we were finally reunited. Since meeting my long-lost twin three years ago, we have kept in regular touch. I've met his family members and his beloved Tughrul Tower, the monument which led to our meeting.

When he says a prayer for me or my family, I can feel it in the depth of my being. Broken parts of our hearts, mended by a flight. A chair that wouldn't recline, a chance encounter, and a reunion of twins.

Out beyond ideas of wrongdoing and right doing,

there is a field. I'll meet you there.

When the soul lies down in that grass,

the world is too full to talk about.

Ideas, language, even the phrase 'each other'

doesn't make any sense.

-Rumi

WITH GRATITUDE

Thank you, first and foremost, to all the wonderful people who have made the stories in The Tapestry of Life come true through thread and word.

Thank you for allowing me to share a moment in your lives; thank you for allowing the beautiful friendships to take form and grow. This could not have happened if I was on this journey alone.

Some of the stories are stories of friendships and encounters between me and animals. I want to thank Mother Earth for making these realities come true.

As far as putting the book together, I want to thank Miriam Osman for her diligence in bringing the stories together.

Thanks to Ayah Rashid for reading through the manuscript and giving me her honest input.

DEEP GRATITUDE

Thank you to Sara Crawford who has so meticulously edited this entire manuscript. I am truly grateful for her expertise and heartfelt edits.

I would also like to thank my friend and travel companion Raz, who has been a source of Light since the beginning on this journey. She truly has given my words flight and for that I will eternally be thankful.

I would also like to thank Green Graphic Design Company for bringing my words together with the images of rugs and tapestries in a way that they intertwine and tell the stories in such a meaningful way.

Finally, my deepest gratitude to my lovely family; Emad, Ariana, and Hannah, who have been with me all along as I had my encounters. I thank you for all your support in helping with the completion of this book. Each of these stories is woven into the tapestry of my life and, therefore, our lives.

BIOGRAPHY

Dr. Bahareh Amidi is a poetry therapist who believes words and voice can be instrumental in the healing process. She holds a master's degree in Family, Marriage and Child Counseling Psychology from College of Notre Dame, and a Ph.D. from Catholic University in Educational Psychology. She completed her Certification in Poetry Therapy at the California-based Institute for Poetic Medicine.

She has worked both in the USA and the Middle East. In Abu Dhabi, she worked with youth, ladies in shelters, victims of human trafficking and men in labor camps. In Tehran she focused predominantly on cancer patients in children's hospitals.

Dr. Amidi has also worked in Silicon Valley with top venture capitalists and numerous corporations. The common factor is always a piece of paper, a pen and a way into the heart. The results are often a drop of tear, a flash of insight, a smile and a self-sustained journey on the path of healing.

Currently she lives in Washington, D.C. and is bringing poetry therapy to Sibley Hospital as part of Johns Hopkins Integrative Health Department. During weekly writing sessions, doors are open to doctors, nurses, administrative personal, patients, and caregivers. Amid the COVID-19 pandemic, Dr. Amidi has been leading online poetry therapy sessions through a variety of online platforms.

Photographer: TJ Salg

Index of Rugs & Tapestries

Courtesy of Medallion Rug Gallery

Persian Tabriz

100% Silk
Size: 8'8"x8'8"

Memluk

Size: 8'1"x10'1"

European

Size: 5'6" x 7'2"

Persian Tabriz

Size: 19'9"x19'9"

Serapi

Size: 9'1"x11'10"

Persian Qum

100% Silk
Size: 9'8"x13'6"

Deco

Size: 8'0"x10'0"

Sultanabad

Size: 12'1"x14'10"

Kashmar

100% Silk
Size: 10'0"x13'9"

Persian Tabriz

Size: 12'10"x18'3"

Persian Bakhtiari

Size: 13'4"x17'6"

Spanish

Size: 9'0"x9'11"

Persian Qum

100% Silk
Size: 9'9"x13'5"

Contemporary

Size: 6'2"x8'9"

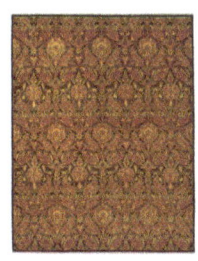

Uzbekistan

Size: 8'1"x10'0"

Khotan

Size: 10'1"x12'9"

Persian Tabriz

Size: 12'9"x18'9"

Persian Qum

100% Silk
Size: 19'3"x33'

Art Deco

Size: 6'1"x8'11"

European

Size: 5'10"x7'9"

Gabbeh

Size: 11'10"x14'8"

European

Size: 4'2"x5'8"

Persian Tabriz

100% Silk
Size: 17'x17'

Uzbekistan

Size: 6'1"x8'9"

Art Deco

Size: 4'2"x5'10"

Kazak

Size: 5'11"x8'3"

Art Deco

Size: 6'0"x8'9"

Persian Esfahan

Size: 13'7"x21'10"

Spanish

Size: 7'11"x9'8"

European

Size: 4'0"x4'0"

Persian Kashan
Size: 9'6"x12'8"

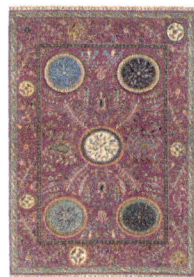
Uzbekistan
Size: 6'11"x9'8"

Art Deco
Size: 9'2"x12'2"

Tabriz
Size: 10'2"x13'2"

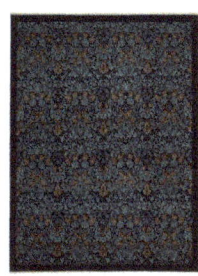
Spanish
Size: 9'0"x11'11"

Uzbekistan
Size: 8'0"x10'0"

Kazak
Size: 7'10"x10'6"

Art Deco
Size: 8'1"x8'4"

Bakhtiari
Size: 13'5"x18'7"

Spanish
Size: 8'1"x10'1"

Persian Qum
100% Silk
Size: 4'5"x6'8"

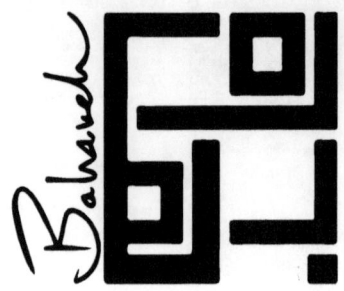

Book Details ISBN The Tapestry of Life
ISBN: 978-0-9974573-1-5 (hardcover)
ISBN: 978-0-9974573-2-2 (paperback)
© Bahareh Amidi. The Tapestry of Life. 2020. All Rights Reserved

connect@bahareh.com	|	www.bahareh.com
facebook.com/BaharehAmidi	|	youtube.com/BaharehLIVE

Also By Bahareh:

The Carousel of Life: Forty Tales Through Poetry and Art
Listen to The Carousel of Life: www.bahareh.com/carousel/

Your Words Your Voice: An Invitation to Expression
Free Download and Video on website
Available on www.bahareh.com

For purchase of books visit **bahareh.com**
or write **connect@bahareh.com**

"The desire to reach the stars is ambitious. The desire to reach hearts is wise and most possible."

Maya Angelou

www.ingramcontent.com/pod-product-compliance
Lightning Source LLC
Chambersburg PA
CBHW061153010526
44118CB00027B/2959